Stone, River, Sky
An Anthology of Georgia Poems

STONE
River
SKY

An Anthology of Georgia Poems

Edited by
CAREY SCOTT WILKERSON
with MELISSA DICKSON

©2015, Negative Capability Press

ISBN 978-0-942544-22-0
Library of Congress Control Number: 2015909402

Publisher/Editor-in-Chief
Sue Brannan Walker

**Associate Publisher/
Creative Director**
Megan Cary

Editor
Carey Scott Wilkerson

Associate Editor
Melissa Dickson

Design Assistants
Lauren McAnally
James Honea Jr.

Cover Photographs
Billy Newman

**Negative Capability Press
Advisory Council**
Carolyn Haines
Roald Hoffman
X.J. Kennedy
Robert Morgan
Marjorie Perloff
Pat Schneider
Robert Morgan
Vivian Shipley

Negative Capability Press was founded in Mobile, Alabama, and has been publishing award-winning books since 1981. Negative Capability Press is a member of APSS: Association of Publishers for Special Sales (formerly SPAN). Wholesale and distribution is available through Small Press Distribution (SPD). For a list of other titles published go to negativecapabilitypress.org.

Negative Capability Press
62 Ridgelawn Drive East
Moble, Alabama 36608

www.negativecapabilitypress.org
facebook.com/negativecapabilitypress

The premise of this book seemed straightforward enough: to assemble a collection of Georgia-inspired poems. To be sure, we expected to find the results fascinating, but we could not have prepared ourselves for the astonishing scope of poetic vision in these pages. Indeed, each poem is both an encounter with the magical properties of a place name and the revelatory document of a personal journey. At the same time, these extraordinary voices together tell a larger story about the importance of poetry itself, its transformative power and its purpose in this strange, beautiful world. The Georgia we witness through these poems is a state of dazzled grace, and to present them here is a privilege indeed.

A special thanks to artist and photographer Billy Newman for his willingness to contribute the photographs upon which the cover art is built. Special thanks also to George Demmy for his wisdom, winning good humor, and hospitality. We must also acknowledge the kind support of our friends, our families, and all the contributors for their patience, good deeds, and splendid work. Finally, deepest gratitude to Sue Walker, Megan Cary, and the staff of Negative Capability Press, without whom none of this would have been possible.

Carey Scott Wilkerson and Melissa Dickson

CONTENTS

Sara Amis
Thirteen Ways of Looking at Black Eyed Peas / 1

Diana Anhalt
Possibilities / 3

Keith Badowski
Out in the Middle of a Field / 4

Rebecca Baggett
Alleluia / 6

Sara Baker
Chihuahua / 9

Marcia Barnes
Tightrope / 11

Laura Beasley
August / 13

Philip Belcher
It's Pronounced [tree-uh n] / 14

Will Blair
From the Canon / 15

Margaret Blake
Folly Island / 17

David Bottoms
Under the Vulture-Tree / 18
Eye to Eye / 19

Deborah Brandon
In Dust What Ties / 20

Jody Brooks
*Complete Conversations with my Father:
Unprovoked and About Which I Am Still Confused* / 21

Jenny Mary Brown
Weekend Strip Club, 1959 / 22

Jericho Brown
On Daniel Minter's High John the Conqueror / 23

Stacey Lynn Brown
My Father Finally Says Out Loud The Word I've Only Heard Him Think / 24

Kathryn Stripling Byer
Heirloom / 25

Brigitte Byrd
Line Shackle 9 / 26

Kevin Cantwell
Syllables on the Problem of Cremation at East Point, Florida / 27

Marian Carcache
Herringbone and Iris / 28

Cathy Carlisi
The Color of Light / 29

Ricks Carson
Upbeat on the Downbeat: A Hymn for Atlanta / 30

Jimmy Carter
A Winter Morning / 33

Katie Chaple
Pretty Little Rooms / 34

Diya Chaudhuri
Dusk / 35

Simona Chitescu
Story in the Late Style of a City / 36

George David Clark
Jellyfish / 37

Jim Clark
Aging Gracefully / 39

Daniel Conlan
Moving Home When that Means to Newnan and You're 25: An Instructional List / 41

Daniel Corrie
Now / 42

Tasha Cotter
Savannah / 43

Bruce Covey
Constellations & Their Meanings / 45

Chad Davidson
Silly / 47

Travis Denton
To a (Buick) Skylark / 48

Melissa Dickson
Taking the Backroads to the Orthodontist / 49

Michael Diebert
Letter to Ferris from Decatur / 50

Maudelle Driskell
Elegy for the Boy I Never Was / 51

Blanche Farley
Mason's Bridge / 52
Laughter / 53

Elizabeth Fields
Wishing On a Star / 54

Rupert Fike
Bacon Grease / 55

Ann Fisher-Wirth
Sundown, Savannah / 56

Gregory Fraser
Against Forgetting Small Towns / 57

Alice Friman
Red Camellia / 58

Lee Furey
Going Back to the River / 59

Elizabeth Garcia
Labor Day, One Year Married / 60

Sarah Gordon
Apertures: Andalusia / 61

Robert Gray
When Skies Are Grey / 63

Beth Gylys
Winter to Spring / 64
Narcissus / 65

Deborah Hall
Silences / 66

Derrick Harriell
Magic City / 67

Pamela Hart
River of Painted Rocks / 68

William Ogden Haynes
Homecoming / 69

M. Ayodele Heath
Father to Son, or A Brief History of Okra (Master's Take) / 70

Graham Hillard
Watching Daybreak on the Savannah / 71

Laurence Holden
What's Needed / 72

Karen Paul Holmes
Poem that Begins with a Definition / 73

H. Holt
Coils of White / 74

Peter Huggins
Woodpecker / 75

Sara Hughes
What You Must Understand / 76

T.R. Hummer
Slow Train Though Georgia / 77

Jamie Iredell
Chattahoochee Low Tide / 78

Robert Perry Ivey
To Home / 79

Mike James
Talking With Allen Ginsberg, In A Dream / 80

Gordon Johnston
Canoe / 82

Melanie Jordan
Apocalypse Tacklebox / 83

Andrea Jurjevic
Cinema Verite: A Love Story / 84
Blackbirds / 85

Lissa Kiernan
Atoms For Peace / 87

Anna King
Like Linen on the Crepe Myrtle / 88

Bill King
Winter Song / 89

Robert S. King
One Man's Profit / 90

Dorothy Knight
The Clermont Lounge, Atlanta GA / 91

Chrissy Kolaya
Savannah / 92

Keetje Kuipers
Georgia / 93

Irene Latham
At Age Ninety My Grandfather No Longer Gardens / 94

Joshua Lavender
Communion / 95

Hank Lazer
N26P49 / 96

Rachel Van Horn Leroy
Georgia Cypress / 97

Kathleen Brewin Lewis
Eggshell / 99

John Lowther
An Unauthenticated Johnny Minotaur Episode Fragment (translated from the Cretan) / 100

Thomas Lux
Fox / 104
The Hunchback Farmhand / 105

Clarence Major
Afternoon Rain / 106
Dangerous Creatures / 107

Christopher Martin
Marcescence / 108

Komal Patel Mathew
Blaming Atlanta / 109

Alan May
Biography of Jimmy Carter / 111

Mariana McDonald
Upon Viewing "Memory as Medicine" / 113

Patrick McGinn
Good Afternoon To Me / 114

Jessica Melilli-Hand
Space Camp Moon-View / 116

Joseph Milford
Holy Porn Tendril / 117

Michael Miller
Singer on River Street, Savannah, Georgia / 120

Judson Mitcham
Weight / 121
Question / 122

Maren O. Mitchell
Learning How to Kill / 123

Sally Stewart Mohney
And What of Camellias / 125

Janice Townley Moore
Evening Out-Atlanta, 1952 / 127

Tony Morris
A Million Fans / 128

Eric Nelson
Georgia Sunset / 130

Jeff Newberry
Prayer after a Rare South Georgia Snow / 131

Laurah Norton
Midshipmen / 132

Nick Norwood
Clamor / 133
The Tie-Snake / 134

Christina Olson
Last Love Letter for Autumn / 135

Lee Passarella
Immanence / 137

Lynn Pedersen
Why We Speak English / 139

Oliver T. Perrin
Tomorrow / 140

Patrick Phillips
Blueridge Bestiary / 141

Stephen Roger Powers
The Mona Lisa in Spain Knows
Why I Can't Come in the Side Door Anymore / 143

Randy Prunty
Vinca Minor / 144

Wyatt Prunty
Two Views / 145

Janisse Ray
Eleventh / 147

Andrea Rogers
The Dupe / 149

Rosemary Royston
Where I'm From / 151

James Sanders
Emory Epiphyte #2 / 152

Mike Saye
Storm Pit / 153

Emily Schulten
Stone Fruit / 154

Ron Self
Romeo and Juliet of the Chattahoochee / 155

Nancy Simpson
My Father Told Me / 157

James Malone Smith
Smartmouth at Large / 158
Smartmouth and The Mysteries / 159

R.T. Smith
Alphabet / 160
Reading Groups / 162

Gregory Vincent St. Thomasino
Mercury / 163
Anselm / 164

John Stephens
Scent of Ash / 165

Todd Stiles
Ghost Train / 166

Leon Stokesbury
Nemerov's "A Primer of the Daily Round" Held as a Mirror Up to Nature / 167
Into the Furthest Regions / 170

Russell Streur
Bicycle Number Nine / 171

Christine Swint
The Red Weaver / 172

Marianne Szlyk
Just a Closer Walk with Thee / 173

Alice Teeter
This Quiet Lake / 175

Jessica Temple
Bearing / 176

Patricia Percival Thomas
Waiting for the Good Humor Man / 178

Jeanie Thompson
Enrico Caruso Remembers Helen Keller / 179

Natasha Trethewey
Carpenter Bee / 180

Meyme Curtis Tucker
Ghosts / 181

Dan Veach
Vale of Soles / 182

Sharon Venezio
Poem in Favor of Driving / 183

J. Phillip Walker
Elegy in the Collapse of a Beautiful Structure / 184

Sue Walker
Threads Out of the Body / 185

William Walsh
Outside Winn Dixie in Suburban Plaza / 186

Theresa Welford
The Bride / 187

Jennifer Wheelock
The Conversation Turns to Wide-Mouthed Jars / 189

Carey Scott Wilkerson
This is Only a Test / 190

M.L. Williams
Summer Thunderstorm / 192

Patricia Williams
Everything Useful I Know About Life I Learned from Margaret Mitchell / *193*

Austin Wilson
Trembling Earth / *194*

Linda Wimberly
Your Voice Surprised Me / *195*

Pete Wingard
Mother Used Only Paper Napkins / *196*

Crystal Woods
On Mondrian's Grave / *197*

William Wright
Grief Map / *198*

Kevin Young
Whole Hog / *200*

Andrew Zawacki
Georgia / *202*

Rebecca Ziegler
Spring Comes to the Coastal Plain / *215*

Contributor's Notes and Biographies / *217*

Sara Amis

THIRTEEN WAYS OF LOOKING AT BLACK EYED PEAS
after Wallace Stevens

I.
Among twenty dishes at a buffet lunch,
The only thing that looked familiar
Was the black eyed peas.

II.
I was of three minds
Like a salad
in which there are kidney beans, chickpeas,
And black eyed peas.

III.
The refried peas rolled up in a tortilla
Were part of a good burrito.

IV.
Peas and cornbread
Are one.
Peas, greens,
And a pan of cornbread
Are one.

V.
I do not know which to prefer,
black eyed peas plain with collards,
or hoppin' john,
the peas with hot sauce,
or with onions, bell peppers, and rice.

VI.
I have leftovers.
What to do? Cold peas as salad,
in salsa, or mashed
into patties and fried?
I may just heat them in the microwave
and eat them late at night.

VII.
O thin women on the television,
Why do you imagine low-fat?
Do you not see that an ounce of fatback
Is worth a pound or two?

VIII.
I know *Mastering the Art of French Cooking*
and how to stir-fry in a wok.
But I know, too,
that black eyed peas are involved
in what I really cook.

IX.
When the black eyed pea is on the grocery shelf
Many different ways, you may find you are in Dixie.

X.
At the sight of black eyed peas
honest in a bowl with cornbread,
Even the celebrity chefs
Would cry out "More!"

XI.
She rode from Georgia to California
On a Greyhound bus.
Once there, she became afraid,
That cowpeas and blackeyed peas
Were not the same and that the cornmeal
Might be of inferior quality.

XII.
It smells like my mother's house.
Black eyed peas must be on the stove.

XIII.
It was supper all afternoon.
I was cooking, and I was going to cook.
The black eyed peas sat simmering
in my crock pot.

Diana Anhalt

POSSIBILITIES

To live without fuchsia, January's sun, Spanish,
smoke-spewing Popocatépetl, the night watchman's
warning whistle, driving both ways on a one-way street
is impossible. *It's who you are, not where you are,*

I tell myself, consoled by thoughts of starting anew:
the dough rising on a floured board, the first rung
of a ladder, Monday mornings, open doors. *So what
am I waiting for?* Fanfares announcing my entrance,

a gust of cold wind, fireworks, applause? No curtain
will rise on me now. I will never leave my footprint
in Atlanta's wet concrete, nor carve my initials
on the trunks of its Chinquapin oaks. Poised

on the shoulders of my former self, I take a deep
breath. Prepare to plunge into tomorrow, a foreign territory.
Study its maps. Drive down Peachtree.

Keith Badowski

OUT IN THE MIDDLE OF A FIELD

a horse grazes a mere stone's roll
from where John Lennon sits on a stool
his hands poised to play his white piano.
My grandma Jaworski wrenches up her face
offended by the horse's stench and
Lennon's Goo *goo g' joob.*
It's strange they should meet this way.
Sinatra throws a drink in Hemingway's face
and then does a handstand and flip
to evade retaliation. I'm eating cherries
straight off a tree when my dead wife
walks up, saying nonchalantly,
They made a mistake. They messed up
my records. I've been alive all this time,
but those doctors never told you.
I'm sure glad she's alive, but I've got to lift
Groucho Marx off the surgical table.
They've amputated his legs.
She helps me heft him onto a cot.
With one hand, Sinatra lights Lennon's cigarette.
With the other, he butchers the former-Beatles'
long hippy locks, using a gigantic pair of scissors.
The horse goes on grazing, making hardly a dent
in the countless miles of green grass.
My dead wife stands nearby, wide eyed
and alive, her pale hands resting on her thighs.
We have so much to say, but we just
look at each other. I wonder if
she can tell how much I've changed.
Lucille Ball consoles the weeping Lennon.
Those bastards . . . They just want me to be
their jukebox! he says.
Sinatra puts the moves on my dead wife.
She smiles that smile she used to flash at me
at him. Their hands meet.
Perhaps it's for the best. So much time

has gone by. We could never get back
to exactly where we left off.
Still I wish someone had told me.
Their bodies are pressed together now.
And they call *that* dancing?
Maybe Sinatra paid off those doctors.
Grandma Jaworski has gone off shopping.
Groucho's got his legs back and
he's is running for President.
Me and Lennon share a candy bar
and watch that horse just go on grazing.

Rebecca Baggett

ALLELUIA

1.

I saw You,
O God,
in the long brown legs
of my daughter
in her fingers that shape
prayers without words

I saw You when she cartwheeled
eight times
across the green field
and rose staggering, panting,
exulting

You shone and shone
like a cartwheel of light
from the body of my brown and joyful girl

2.

And, oh, my daughter's sweet bones
flashing beneath her skin

beneath that thin, taut glaze, that cherished illusion,
the shape of You glowing, glowing

3.

At first I did not know You
in the lank black body
of the roadside tom, rank
with blood and fear.
Like the others, I passed
You by. But I turned back,
although I did not recognize You,
wrapped You in the worn pink blanket
from the back seat. Your blood-filled
eye blinked unsurprised at the blank
and voiceless sky, but I felt
Your heart tremble beneath my hand,
felt the heart's old persistent music,

beyond logic, beyond hope,
and so I heaved You into my car,
and I drove to the veterinarian,
murmuring, "All right, it's all right,
it's all right," though I never
believed it, while Your blood seeped
into the blanket, and Your stench
filled my nostrils, and I prayed

I would not have to touch You again.

Then Your scrabbling feet stilled
to the sound of my voice, and You pushed
your dirty head against my thigh,
and a great purr rumbled
from Your broken chest,
and I knew You,
and You died.

4.

It was a day there was no pain,
though I knew pain would follow,
like an old dog that will not leave,

knew I'd pay for this hour
tramping the banks of the Oconee
with a cold skewer of pain
through my hip and my knee

But it didn't matter. That
was the day I decided
to be happy,

thinking that happiness may be
the only thing You want from us,
the only gift You can use

5.

How else could You have seen
the black dragonfly
dancing over the dark water,
the flash of iridescent blue
beneath its wings, quick
as a breath, how else
could You see the dragonfly dart,
then hesitate above the mossy green
bank as if it gave pleasure
deliberately? How could You perceive
the green dimness falling

between trees, that antique
stillness, then the vermilion leaves,
startling, unexpected, like an exclamation
of delight, how could You receive
that moment when one, then two,
then three dragonflies skimmed
over the Oconee River

except through me
except through me
except through me

Sara Baker

CHIHUAHUA
(after *Starfish*, in homage to Eleanor Lerman)

This is what Life does. It gives you an eleven year old
so innocent he talks about erections as if they are built from leggos,
only with blood and tissue. A child who doesn't want to go through "perversity"
because he doesn't want wet dreams, which Alante and Lucas say are gross,
and who says every night, "I never want to leave you, Mom."

Life gives you a mother who revises history as she goes along,
so the glorious future you grew up with becomes the glorious past
that never was and there is no place for the misery you remember.
You were never sick under her roof and all your ills are because you left her.
The good memories that glimmer like lost coins in the dirt are yours alone,
there is no one to share them with, so you are abandoned not once,
but twice. She erases the chalkboard and starts over,
with houses, clothes, memories, with you.

But then, Life suggests to you that you don't have to live with her anymore,
you can go to the sauna instead. Where another woman, older and tireder
than you, sits in companionable silence and sighs, both of you unashamed
of your striated bellies that have flowered and fruited and now simply sit on your
thighs contentedly, where you breath in the cedar darkness, the heat like love
moving deeper and deeper into your tissues, the heat wrapping itself
around you so that all feels forgiven.

And then Life lets you meet your innocent son outside the sauna and take your
not-so-painful back to Walgreens where two queenly black ladies in hats
complain about how their pastor is driving them to drink
and a young woman on a cell phone tells her friend about a hawk
that grabbed her Chihuahua.
You imagine the dog lifting off into the sky,
its eyes glistening with terror,
the girl's hands snatching back its trembling body.

Then Life lets you go home. Where, even though your
back hurts again, you cook your favorite dinner for your
daughter and her boyfriend, whom you like very much,

and you drink a little too much wine and you reflect
that you could have been like that Chihuahua, that life
could have been a hawk and sunk its talons into your hide
but instead something reached up and caught you and pulled you
back to earth. And then you smile at your old love across the table,
the one who would do until something better came along, though
now you know there is nothing better, and you help yourself
to another piece of pie.

Marcia Barnes

TIGHTROPE

July in the mountains,
heat oppressive
with thirty thousand
assembled near the gorge.

Men and children
hanging off the rocks;
politicians worked the crowd.
All came to see Wallenda walk.

A wiry man, not much
above five feet tall,
came to Georgia to walk the sky,
and cross Tallulah Gorge.

What makes a man do these things?
Is it money, or maybe pride?
No. Wallenda came to walk the gorge.
That's all.

An eerie silence fell
as he stepped on the wire.
Reverend Turpin said a prayer,
"Lord, just keep them feet a-walking."

Seven hundred feet above
rocks and rushing water
Wallenda stopped his steady steps
not once, twice, and never faltered.

He stopped to do a headstand
to prove that he could do it,
and then, to keep a promise
for the boys away at war.

The man walked twenty minutes,
held a pole weighing thirty pounds,

and people stared with wonder
'til Wallenda was on the ground.

What prayer was on his lips?
Or did he hear Papa saying,
"Life is on the wire,
the rest is just waiting."

Laura Beasley

AUGUST

You were diagnosed
when the plums and peaches
at the grocery store were ripest,
when the beefsteak tomato vines
by our backyard fence
broke from too much fruit.

The doctor showed us slides
of your cells multiplying
in some inexplicable frenzy.
And a hurricane hit the tip of Florida.
We watched on your hospital TV.
Waves swelled over a beach
as you tried to sleep, palms white,
head rolled back, mouth opened.

I remember our father told us
about that time he served
as an official witness from the press
to an execution in Alabama,
back when they still used the chair.

And the hardest part of writing
the story, he said, was reporting
the last meal—bacon cheeseburgers,
milkshakes, fried chicken,
an omelet, apple pie—how
the prisoner had been too scared to eat.

Philip Belcher

IT'S PRONOUNCED [tree-u*h n*]

I love the *Antiques Road Show*—how its treasures
confound or confirm my intuition, how smart
the latter makes me feel, how it flays
my idea of value: the rickety old rocker is
worth $10,000; the Tiffany lamp a fake.
And in Savannah, how the empty wooden box
the size of a card deck—a chipped mosaic
on its lid (I'd have tossed it in the fire, fed
it to the stove)—turns out to be Tunbridge Ware
(as if I know what that means) and valued
by the twin appraisers at enough to pay my mortgage
for a year. It doesn't even yield the needles
and thread it was meant to bear, its purpose
irrelevant, its maker's intent dismissed.

Will Blair

FROM THE CANON

If I were Cummings,
I'd write of your thighs
our flesh, my desire.

Of penetration.

If I were Donne,
I'd write of your spirit
our kingdom, my rapture.

Of hue.

If I were Poe,
I'd write of your darkness
our thunder, my insanity.

Of phantoms.

If I were Wilde,
I'd write of your masks
our complexity, my hypocrisy.

Of borderlands.

If I were Miller,
I'd write of your sex
our sex, my sex.

Of sex.

If I were Whitman,
I'd write of your hope,
our immortality, my fall.

Of liberation.

If I were Kerouac,
I'd write on and on and on.

Of libations.

But it's just me,
so I don't know
what to write.

Margaret Blake

FOLLY ISLAND

Canted sunlight punctures
Spanish moss: a hammered
tin lantern of late afternoon.

Hawks angle sharp, the nibs
of fountain pens, as whelk shells
wear to the last internal spiral.

Every ten feet, slight birds fluster
into sky again, hoping for absence
when they land at my feet.

None of the starfish are dead
enough to take home, broken quahogs
gleam purple, mauve, even a dirty

yellow, my need for shells stuttering
my footprints across tide lines, while
finally tired, the lighthouse rusts.

Paint sloughs, littering salt water,
as dead panes count and recount
old nights they crowded with safety.

David Bottoms

UNDER THE VULTURE-TREE

We have all seen them circling pastures,
have looked up from the mouth of a barn, a pine clearing,
the fences of our own backyards, and have stood
amazed by the one slow wing beat, the endless dihedral drift.
But I had never seen so many so close, hundreds,
every limb of the dead oak feathered black,

and I cut the engine, let the river grab the jon boat
and pull it toward the tree.
The black leaves shined, the pink fruit blossomed
red, ugly as a human heart.
Then, as I passed under their dream, I saw for the first time
its soft countenance, the raw fleshy jowls
wrinkled and generous, like the faces of the very old
who have grown to empathize with everything.

And I drifted away from them, slow, on the pull of the river,
reluctant, looking back at their roost,
calling them what I'd never called them, what they are,
those dwarfed transfiguring angels,
who flock to the side of the poisoned fox, the mud turtle
crushed on the shoulder of the road,
who pray over the leaf-graves of the anonymous lost,
with mercy enough to consume us all and give us wings.

EYE TO EYE

Suddenly I noticed the silence – the robins, jays, mockingbirds
all gone quiet, the cardinals and song sparrows quiet.

Then as Jack and I turned onto the homeward loop of our walk,
the sky startled us with a shriek –

two hawks circling above the pines, screaming from tree to tree,
two hawks from the heavy nest

above our neighbor's house, screaming then going silent
in the branches of a Bradford Pear.

We crossed under that tree and stopped to catch
the larger hawk, the female, eye to eye.

Jack sat by the curb and stared. I stared.
And head cocked, leaning forward, she stared, incredulous,

working her jaw, quietly, nervously.
I made faces, snarled, bared my teeth, and the hawk

never flinched. Only stared until those orange inflamed eyes
became the terrible jaundiced eyes of my father

that final moment he raised his lids.
(The silenced voice tells the truth.)

Like my father's jaw, her jaw trembled.

Deborah Brandon

in dust what ties

        one thing to an other?
        low-slung sky &&

        squatting trees
        poles carrying
        a path / who has walked?

        stumps, stubbles
        one tree caught
        swayyying

        a house like a shy child
        shrinking
        no shield
        branches sturdy
        things fall

        through
        && no piece of dust
        stays the same
        place for long

                                    you see already we have *past*
                                          she is no part of
                                              this present

Jody Brooks

COMPLETE CONVERSATIONS WITH MY FATHER: UNPROVOKED AND ABOUT WHICH I AM STILL CONFUSED

Dad: "You remember Uncle Snooze?"
Me: "No."
Dad: "He lived over where I shot that deer in the ass. Had a great swimming pool."

D: "You ever hear of Goat Man?"
M: "Not that I recall."
D: "He used to live up in that cove. They called him Goat Man because he came down from the mountains once a month with his cart and his goats. I never knew what he was selling, but people always had to go see him about something."

D: "You ever meet Bang Bang LaFarr? Guy that sold chicken diapers?"
M: "I don't understand any part of that question."
D: "Bang Bang, sold chicken diapers. You know, the absorbent pads at the bottom of styrofoam chicken containers. He sold those."

D: "You remember Iva, Charlie's mother?"
M: "Vaguely."
D: "When we were kids, Charlie covered his walls with Playboy pin-ups. Iva cut out party dresses for every one of those ladies and pinned them on when they had company. She was proud of that."

D: "You remember Tommy and Wayne?"
M: "Kind of."
D: "Every day, same time, they'd carry their foldout chairs to the grassy spot beside the depot and watch the train go by. Then they'd fold them up and go home. That's the way to do it."

D: "You remember what your great grandmother used to do?"
M: "Tell me."
D: "She used to wait for the nurse to go on rounds and she'd play dead. The nurse would lean down close, real close to check for breath and Granny Tom would say 'Boo.' Crazywoman. You never knew what would come out of her mouth."

Jenny Mary Brown

WEEKEND STRIP CLUB, 1959

My great uncle Mike, late in the evening,
snuck upstairs to cross-dress, returning

in false eyelashes and a satin pink shift.
Trumpets brought him back downstairs

in a beige Playtex Cross-Your-Heart bra,
high heels, and jet black panties, flirting

with his wife, his brothers, tossing
shed garments to the whooping crowd.

The basement bar, now filled with cans
of tomatoes that I stack and re-stack, held

Tanqueray for Tom Collins and posters
of mostly nude women pasted to the wall:

Legs uncovered, breasts blurred by bottles,
swooping blonde curls tossed over

bare shoulders, cherry-puckered lips,
a few feathers, sequins, and white lace–

They're still here now under a hanging
light bulb, painted into beach scenes

or on a park bench, red umbrellas in hand.
With corners peeling off the walls, they've

outlived uncle Mike. Smiling, eyebrows
arched; pink fingers still lifting hemlines.

Jericho Brown

ON DANIEL MINTER'S HIGH JOHN THE CONQUEROR
acrylic, 50x60 cm

The sun inflicts its whitest light, heat
High enough to warp the pavement,
So John gives up on the new road north
And cuts through red clay at first sight
Of shade, barbed wire broken, miles
Of green to be cleared or cleaned growing
In rows like welts behind him. God's
Not on his side. John won't work
A whole day and can't keep cancer
Out his mouth. Oh, he's got the shoulders
For it, the stride, arms and hands
The size of a laboring man's, but one
Itch for smoke in his throat and John
Heads for hell. Nothing about Georgia
Can slow him down. King of all
That slithers, here he chokes a snake.
I catch his yellow eye and remember
My own pack of menthols, days I'd drag
And puff lies in front of my wife who
Waited while I wished for man after man,
Black in two dimensions, to run my way,
Dear John, a region painted against me.

Stacey Lynn Brown

MY FATHER FINALLY SAYS OUT LOUD THE WORD I'VE ONLY HEARD HIM THINK

Calling it a *rehab center* doesn't change
this nursing home, doesn't daub dry the drool
or bring the unfocused wheelchair bound back
from those sepia grained memories half
a century ago, gentleman callers in stiff suits
clutching flowers they never brought, doesn't hush
the hollerers or still the worrying hands
of the woman in the corner who asks me for a peach
every time I pass her, every day for weeks
until the day her chair is empty, the day
I stand outside my father's room, listening
as he argues with the Kenyan caregivers, resisting
their pleas for him to cooperate, roll over, *please*
let them clean the messy sheets that shame him when suddenly
through the garbled spit of catfish that used to be
his language, I hear the word peal clean and sharp, serrating
the spaces between them, hanging in the air
like a curtain to be parted, and I walk through, chirping
cheerfully, smiling apologetically to the two women
who scurry out, exchanging glances between them
as my father looks up at me with rheumy eyes
I might mistake for tears if it had been the aphasia,
if the wrong word had come out at the wrong time,
unsummoned, but no, it wasn't. Not this time.

Kathryn Stripling Byer

HEIRLOOM

We never doubted the hoop
in which we cast our stories would hold
fast, the stitches we made
last as long we held the cloth steady.
Not once did we heed the underside
whereon the knots gnarled their own story,
nubby as scars from a wound
or a welt left behind by a switch.

We never doubted our own fingers
threading the tendrils of mercerized cotton
through steel eyes, each licked tip
we pushed through as small
as the lint we launched into the bedrooms
when we shook the weathered chenille,
settling itself on the carpet like dandruff

she scraped from our scalps
every dusk with such ruthless care
we could hear the Big Dipper ringing
the night's bucket. No lice.
Not even the tiniest nit. Thankful,
we sank into feather beds,
blessing each other, the chickens,
the mules, even sows at the trough,

knowing we had been scrubbed
clean as ever we would be,
our nails clipped,
our noses blown,
every black signet of dirt pried
from under our fingernails.
The window fans blowing
their currents through passageways,
hummed like the treadle of God stitching
the fabric we called home, the earth
drawing over us its heirloom of dust.

Brigitte Byrd

LINE SHACKLE 9

If I look in the mirror, and it's not a metaphor, I see a woman whose husband chops Florence fennel and Anjou pears in the afternoon while she plants the seeds of imagination in my head under vanity lights. Transported to the field of artifice, and extravagance, I alter the litany of I's with elaborate visions. I am two women echoing each other. Our lips curl funny like in comics strips when the desire for comedy shows up into a crooked smile. Shall we lavish on the subject of the aging woman?

If she is a broken woman under a black sun, dark circles and hooded eyes to fit her misery, and her age, stories plowed deep into the skin to leave their mark on her face, I ask her fingers to knead the cheeks upward into ripples, tap under the chin to restore the jaw line. She greets my efforts to cheer her up and reshape her face with a saturnine expression. "Too much skin," she says, and I take refuge in passive denial until the husband steps in the picture, eyes red with tears. Soon what appears to be empathy to fill the afternoon's melodrama turns into buffoonery when he says, "I can't remember that trick to chop onions without crying."

If she is a composed woman in the midst of another heat tsunami sweeping over her décolletage, the neck, the upper lip, cheeks and ears, skin flushed ardent red, I recall the practical husband's gift of three hand fans when I hear something about chopping onions without crying and know I owe him an explanation. "Keep your mouth shut!" I say as his perplexed face slips in the mirror, wet eyed and runny nosed, and we decide on splashing water on our faces to regain our composure.

If she is a compassionate woman who just read Julia Kristeva when she sees the crying husband in the mirror, and she hears Flaubert whine for attention, I say, "Can regret be beautiful?" which, somehow, the dog interprets as "Shall we go for a walk?" The canine slip sets off effective tail wagging, a welcomed breeze, nails click-clacking on the wooden floor. Feigning not to rejoice at the happy ending to the chopping saga, the husband shifts his blurred gaze from the onions to Flaubert, rescuer extraordinaire, running toward us like Hermes, the bringer of good luck, and he says, "Is it time for a walk?" and, magically, I know to drop the matter and slip on my earthly sandals.

Kevin Cantwell

SYLLABLES ON THE PROBLEM OF CREMATION AT EAST POINT, FLORIDA

      For this kind of fun, they cheat the gulls of bread,
and throw bits of shell, by which they are called back down.
      This trick gets them one short laugh of the day.
They are so broke too they do not have one more thing left
      to touch but their own cold hands
shoved in their pants, and the seams that are sewn folds
      like the tops of seed bags, though not one black seed
clings to the duff of that lint.

      The gulls know it is not bread, yet they are so poor
they peck at it while it falls. And then these two men
      try once more to show how lean
a week can get with no check, or how the wind will push
      the gray sea to them, and how the gulls
will veer hard, cut through the wind, and if it is
      that time of day, the gray, tin, near side of their wings
will flash as they rise back up.

      And if this hour looks like the end,
they have come, from up at the house, where it's been hard
      all day, where they have called their friends
who will not hang up, folks they have owed
      cash from day one, or a car ride or junk for when
those things scratched their need. Now they must
      have more to put their old mom to her last bit of ash,
plus the bill for the gas touched to a white blaze

      —and more for at least a waxed box,
or a blue jar, which they have no place to keep or set,
      the house not hers, but just for these
last months, for her mail, a straight chair in the yard,
      the grass not cut, one path to the pale car, one to the sea,
where her two sons fool a bird and make its slow kin
      turn in the high wind, where one more time they must drop down
in the awful tongues of the Pentecost.

Marian Carcache

HERRINGBONE AND IRIS

Between the blue Nivea tin and the silver crucifix
an amber glass powder box,
kept Eugenia's white hair.
Every night she removed tortoise combs
to brush it a hundred strokes
and place those strands that floated loose
inside Iris and Herringbone.

One day when I was ten
she brewed a cup of Red Diamond tea so strong it was almost black,
hung her head over the sink,
and anointed herself a redhead again at eighty-nine.

I used to throw my hair to birds;
Aunt Shabie saved hers so enemies couldn't work a hex;
I never asked Eugenia why.
Tonight I wish I had her long-lost hair,
that still-tangible part of her.

Delicate Iris, sturdy Herringbone,
the powder box sits on my dresser now –
seems to draw moonbeams on this southern summer night –
and holds my hair,
thick and brown with highlights as red as Georgia clay:
A gift from Eugenia.

Cathy Carlisi

THE COLOR OF LIGHT

What is chlorophyll
but sunlight translated
into a different tongue?
Grass calls it emerald,
oak leaves—sap green.
The way it smacks
the lip of each ripple
in a creek–the creek
screams white. Squint
hard, and yellow light
gets pinked by blood.

Sit by a window, and its
the headlines or Kafka
or a thin lavender thread poking
through a needle's eye.

To the painter, sunlight is
every slick stick of straw,
each fold of burnt bark.
It's crimson clay, gray
and phthalo veins
on a hand's back.

To me, light is her walking
toward me in the grass
beneath the leaves.

Ricks Carson

UPBEAT ON THE DOWNBEAT: A HYMN FOR ATLANTA

Chaos is a theory. Love is a fact.

I heard a voice utter in the halfdark
don't let anybody tell you the city
doesn't wipe blood some call a sunrise
off its morning mouth
that spent the night bouncing
from clubs across the pavement
while bitches in stilettos
and sequins clicked around the wound
and grinned to see the fists
clenched to crack a jaw.
They turned soon enough to things
it was sumptuous to introduce
at points of entry, their bodies
being no less cagey than a mouse
that never has just one hole or a killer
with his six-cylinder rampage in his hand.
But morning is the time of breaking
down the rules of night that hid Venus
and uncovering light from brutal bones
in gutters, those freeways of the roach and rat,
those open veins of the streets
influxed with rock or horse
and convulsed with the grimace of bliss;
and the bones teeter up and sway
into dew that the dawn seraphs wrapped
in ethereal mists and caused to bead up
on the forehead of the sinful ground
so a christening sun could turn
the drops into baptismal fires
and burn beauty into the auroral wreck.

So much for the simple body, the voice said,
but what about the soul abraded
on the pavement and patchy with scabs?

Look, I said, see the tiny white lappings of halo
at the edges of the wounds
like morning on the roofs?
And if you run across a loose specter
sniffing the pavement for its body
that left the soul outside while it went
into a house of Ill Good Repute,
consider it was of the soul's obligation
to bear the laws on its back
as if etched like Moses' tablet.

Love is nocturnal, a cat that licks
the streetlights off the streets
and chases it with rat-blood
until it glows and sets the teeth
of dogs and men on edge,
from whose mouths burst forth
'O Lord the angel death is upon us,'
marauding the alleys and setting
steeples ablaze all over this city God
forgot to rain down fire and brimstone upon,
whose homeless huddle in kudzu huts
while the rich eat salvation on grilled toast points
despite coyotes slouching past their gated doors
and will leave cleanpicked bones
of poodles and fat cats at garage doors
behind which the Mercedes shrink
in German angst, o mein Gott
sei neben, but He is too far gone
in the Heavens among the River of Lifers
to turn his eye toward the gated backyards
of three-piece suits and tennis skirts.

Yet holy indeed are the wires
taut above the streets. Our
God is hip in his groove now
the Greatest of Electricians,
angels doing loop-de-loops
throughout the hoops men in cherrypickers
and yellow beetlehats wove in the phone lines
like perfected Etch-a-Sketch tracery
so the eastwest and northsouth circuits
linking heaven to earth and earth to souls
might hum to the birds clinging to them

that fight off the wind with puffed breasts,
whose heads bear crowns of early sun.
So you want to know love,
really know love, know real love,
it is here you must arch your hearts
and eyes upward, to the sky
that twice has given itself to us
and twice has been spurned.
O Atlanta, city of bloodied mouths,
city of hollowedout eyes and hopes,
city of false morning fiascos of haste,
I who am abandoned in the midst,
slowmoving and berated,
have read your palm in cracked pavement
the pimps tread their supple leather boots on,
but you city cannot see yourself quivering
in rainmirrors, cannot see yourself
filling slowly with wounded light
and splendor of the holy ghost
tossing dice, against all odds, to win you.

Jimmy Carter

A WINTER MORNING

My father's touch would end my childish dream,
fitful as it was. This venture off with him
was entry into the grownup world for me.

I snuggled near him, cold wind in my face
until our pickup reached the proper place.
While still too dark for us to see

we heard the killdeer and a long bob-white
as bird songs prophesied the end of night.
It was as near to heaven as could be.

We waited, anxious, till the brightening sky
showed other hunters at their stands nearby.
Guns began to fire, and doves to die.

Katie Chaple

PRETTY LITTLE ROOMS

> *—The remains of who was thought to be the Renaissance poet Francesco Petrarch are instead those of two different people, DNA tests have confirmed.*

The skull was unexpected, a surprise in the pink marble tomb.
In 1873, the old doctor of Padua claimed it had crumbled,
as though too injured to live outside that stone room.
Did he keep it on his desk? On his shelf as a specimen,
an exemplar of perfection, the knitted plates
a symbol of all that we cannot know of love?

The doctor was not the only man who needed—a friar fled
his flagged cell, hacked off the poet's arm, spirited it back,
a drunk friar in such grief for the world, so moved
as to steal the physical. And where and how to keep it—
this limb that had once moved to love's measure?

And now, these scientists with their test tubes, their milliliters
and tweezers are used to wounds and hairs, blood
and shatter. In their white coats and labs, they don't ask
questions they don't know the answers to. They brush
away quarry dust, measure the circumference, count the alleles,
and approximate the years—all equating female.
Nobody asks: Whose body was not loved enough
that her skull could travel like a pebble,
could be used to punctuate the line of a man's body?

Diya Chaudhuri

DUSK

Already, a doddering chair has given way beneath me:
I am five points of contact with the earth.
Already, I'm a drunken clinging to the elbow
of an editor from a press no one can quite

recall at the moment. We're all speechless at the thought
of raccoons already, and more importantly, of raccoon hands
which, all agree — wide-eyed and scanning the yard —
are alarming. More calming: two roosters

with the run of this farm. If I squint through
the darkening by tiki torch flicker, I make out a woman
slowing toward them, a single finger unsheathed before
her, an epee for the prodding of noble breasts.

The roosters tease close enough to eavesdrop,
and pick at crumbs fallen from paper plates, but loiter
just there, out of lunging, catching, or clutching
to one's bosom's reach. More cooperative by far,

an unnamed and breedless puppy — all cartilage,
soft bones, and upturned belly — who cyclones
the yard the length of the night in search of hands.
Too many hands, though, time being limited

to a single night. Like a fish in strong current, he's in
his element: slick, instinctive, un-snared as of yet.
Captive: a mother hen, her teenaged brood,
a moth – tormented, a tragic hero in a ring

of snapping beaks who's not yet thought to fly *up* –
and three slurring women, our noses to chicken
wire, fingers looped through, calling for
the others to come witness the spectacle.

Simona Chitescu

STORY IN THE LATE STYLE OF A CITY
after Larry Levis

There are elusive signs in everything. Lilac trees
spring up like giants, color and scent, a language
of survival in the absence of fruit. The streets grow quiet
for a few hours, before the bustle of women bargaining
prices for mackerel, rainbow trout, lemons, olives,
before bakers snap their fingers, fill the window
displays with éclairs and profiteroles, in rows as precise
as a Securitate platoon. Stillness is substance in this cathedral
of symbols: in the winter, a frozen river, in the summer,
clusters of wine-red cherries weighing down branches.
Such deceptive plenty everywhere. We didn't need meat, or sugar,
or an appetite. Come summer, the markets brimmed, come winter,
we ice skated through blizzards, through snowflakes delicate
as goose feathers. Our skin peeled, we had frost bite, we knew
that kind of happiness. Armies marched and civilians marched.
Tanks came through the city in silent convoys. The roads were covered
in snow, in trash, in petals, in grief. In times of misfortune the soul
makes tenderness of its wounds. Chooses its analogies.
Today we are a still-life of silver winged fish, dressed with persimmons,
watermelon. Tomorrow, a tableaux vivante of hunting rites.
The city belongs to no one in this crescendo light of day.
Today we wake up children, tomorrow we are the state official
who once invited a beggar in his loge to listen to *Carmen*,
and the beggar wept, saying he had never rested on such soft seats.

George David Clark

JELLYFISH

The dark sea dreams them.
They are the unexchangeable
currency of dreams,

the interest the other world
pays and pays into this one.
In the pre-dawn blue

they seem hewn out
from the littoral like great
waterlogged diamonds,

an interior gleam.
Who speaks for them
speaks for the secret

side of the womb,
for they are the long-tasseled
death-bonnets of children

we conceive but never
bring to term. And so we love
and jointly curse them.

It is impossible now
to tell if they reach for us
or we for them, so strange

is their volatile gravity.
They are sisters
to the moon then, and pulse

in her wake, a curdled
blooming of echoes
as she too is an echo.

But in the fluorescent pink
and green pockets
of their bodies, softer

than night, they're smuggling
rumors of suns we fail
to imagine. They hold

whole oceans beneath
their umbrellas. Tell me,
friend, is there an end

to revelation? The poison
flowers blossom inside us
like Rorschachs

we might believe in.
Evening and thunderheads
in the austral sky,

the jellyfish tides,
an exhibition of lightnings
and scaled-down Hiroshimas:

if they proceed
like messengers,
another breed of angel,

then it falls on us to hear
and heed them,
their cold medusa-bells

resounding, calling us
back through the black
sand of sleep.

Jim Clark

AGING GRACEFULLY

We are men, in our late thirties,
and we have set the neighbor's roof afire.
"Flaming balls," the packages read,
crude lettering provocatively purpling
the flimsy cardboard, shrink-wrapped and
innocently lying in their silver-dusty bin
at Big Ed's State Line Fireworks Supermarket,
Chattanooga, TN. The inscrutable logo
should have warned but didn't: A lone rocket
atop a pair of cherry bombs.

Now, in this sultry suburb of the city
Sherman burned, the last gleam of twilight
fading in the west, to the fevered delight
of our attendant offspring we have
lit the fuse, and we have run away.

Independence flowers overhead, reflected
in our wistful eyes. Seconds later,
a woman's voice calls from the porch "I see
something over there. A light. There,"
We turn as one, and there – *There!* –
the loose shag of dry pine needles littering
the neighbor's roof erupts in fiery cascade.

In the acrid dark we clamber over chain-link
as tall as a man – slip, rip, howl and we are in.
Someone is pulling a bucking, sputtering hose
through a chain-link diamond, and in my stomach
beer loses ground to flaming Hot Wings, the inner
world mirroring the outer. Through mist and smoke
and lurid flame dimly I see three figures
on the roof, stomping out flames, sweating,
bent double. Some herky-jerky Outback ritual
dance unfolds, complete with rhythmic chant –
Anybody home? Oh, Anybody home! – and I think
I must be dreaming.

                          Stillness. Startled silence.
Then bodies, damp and smudged, slide from the roof.
Show's over. Nobody's home. Wind in the empty garden
hose moans like a didgeridoo.
The fire truck slunk back to the station.
The Sheriff let us off with a warning.
The neighbors came home drunk and didn't notice.
The women put the children to bed and talked
low on the porch, long into the night. We knew
to stay away. Sometime later on a breath of wind
came the chuckled whisper – "Flaming Balls!"

Daniel Conlan

MOVING HOME WHEN THAT MEANS TO NEWNAN AND YOU'RE 25
An Instructional List

Think of this place only as a space with too few bars. Prepare to drive familiar streets, past a museum that seemed never open when you were interested, past houses old enough to mean unburnt in Georgia and everyday to see your father's car. Forget and forget counting. Prepare to hear "There's no shame [in living with your mother]" and learn it's so. Make excuses (wrong-place-wrong-time, underemployment statistics, predatory lending, etc.) all subprime, none a reason. Don't accept excuses. Exercise patience while driving: use your horn, gesture, but don't yell yourself hoarse as someone refuses to turn left on red onto and from a one-way. Take your car to it's home service station which was a BP before and its fuel affiliation now, forget; know there will be no mechanic anxiety. Prepare to offer people you once knew or knew of a knowing smile and nod in the grocery store: don't no-look, know you will no-look. Learn not to look for implications (boy-man, arrested development, etc.) in "millennial." Occasionally work in your mother's yard. Be emotionally available. Be willing to forge new experience. Avoid old digs, old judgments. Avoid the paper's "Community Forum" or prepare for blood pressure meds. Walk around with headphones in your ears. Pick a piece of sidewalk: remember then and list the differences. In public, speak only to people you've never met before. Celebrate the lack of bars and, therefore, the lack of guilt for only ever going to one. Don't remember high school. Forget the high school's tennis courts and its tantrums. Forget humiliations suffered; those inflicted, only enough to avoid repetition. Avoid any "reunion" especially unofficial and at the court square's dive, an old theater with its marquee reading down two stories from the top: The Alamo. As in remember: avoid saying too much, avoid drinking too much, avoid saying "forget The Alamo," say too much, avoid self-judgment. Don't take advice. Offer advice. Be alone. Enjoy a screened porch and enjoy screen time. Be emotionally unavailable. Sit on a swing. Sit on a glider. People watch. Drink less. Refuse any social function that requires etiquette. Be kind. Forget that you've ever lived here before. Remember losing your father's Boy Scout knife in the ivy four houses down. Know you have lost–forget this list. Shoot hoops and play tennis; remember losing to your father: those miracles of wile and poise.

Daniel Corrie

NOW

The NASA camera's shutter
blinked, time and deep space
kept in the now of a page,
great blackness of night's
stars eddying into stars,
the small, indifferent spirals
swallowing themselves,
galaxies drifting away
from galaxies to farther night's
moment always closing
toward a moment's opening,
single moment of all place
emerging from all place
into a farther place that is all,
inflections and immensities
continuing, a lone pulsar
strobing, lost somewhere far
in the photograph, its throb
measuring each interval
reshaping to a newer interval,
night washing over a beach,
breakers combing hair to white
in moonlight's salty rinse,
where I feel myself rising
to stand in sand, faltering
shoreward, pulled and pushed
in wave-heave then wave-heave,
knowing my now as a feeling,
my years' memories swimming
through now's forgetfulness
of eons' moments swarming
more than all swarming stardust,
vivid pivot-point of presence
like the dolphin glimpsed
in its leap through arc of air,
like surf reaching to receding,
like a breath into a breath,
like an eye's eclipsing blink,
primordial newness always
vanishing through becoming
the ancient suddenness of now.

Tasha Cotter

SAVANNAH

> *The drawing of an eclipse does not demand any great artistry*
> *[on the other hand] there is something enigmatic about an eclipse.*
> "On the Marionette Theatre"
> Heinrich von Kleist

I cannot remember the name of that
bay area town, but it buzzed
with Spring crowds, banners,
and the seafood was cheap,
quick, and fast to finish.

As Georgia sat on its thumbs
tapping its foot to live jazz
scratching a black dirty chest:
farmer in drought.
Grey smoked eyes widening with the disbelief

of good invention. Sounds of an old bay area,
sounds of an eclipsed era.

      Oh, yes near the water, an island
town. Not Atlanta, not suburb
and the park steps led right into the
ocean serving as a carpet to
the drifting boats

tugged by the water, and brushed by bitter salt.
The breeze was cold, but I was given

a sweet grass tulip now behind my door,
a sappy mess of canola. And though
yellowed, it still speaks to me in
waves, the beach not forgotten, the boats
not harbored, the music not resting. Any twist
and knot has avoided time.

      Now so many spent. The town
compressed to the cream

as the oceanside city expands.
The only art left is the sedentary boat hum.
So, for my own epigraph:

"The blue is all I listened to."

Bruce Covey

CONSTELLATIONS & THEIR MEANINGS

Andromeda: When red dust pours out of your slashed wrist.
Antlia: What protrudes from a doe's head.
Apus: A single feline.
Aquarius: Once associated with morning.
Bootes: Two German war films, shaken not stirred.
Caelum: All the cakes & wines have a sacred air.
Camelopardalis: A slow-moving cat creature with a hump.
Cancer: From the French, unable to speak.
Canis: Chasing Apus.
Carina: One of my favorite NY poets.
Casseopeia: Punished by the Nymphs to appear forever as a W.
Circinus: Containing three rings.
Corvus: The lower, narrow portion of the uterus.
Crux: The outside part of a loaf of bread.
Dorado: An unelevated automobile.
Equuleus: A vacuum designed to suck up horsehair.
Fornax: Illegal in 36 states.
Gemini: Tiny minerals.
Grus: What grass does or did.
Horologium: The art of planting gems.
Hydra: A worldwide subversive organization dedicated to world domination.
Indus: A series of statues sculpted from ink.
Lacerta: An injury received from a laser beam with fresh breath.
Leo: Aka, "the Lip." Managed the Dodgers from 39-46 & 48.
Mensa: Thinks it's smarter than it really is.
Microscopium: Not worth worrying about.
Monoceros: Bored or boring.
Musca: Smelly or smelling.
Norma: A tragic opera in two acts by Vincenzo Bellini.
Octans: The amount of "oomph" in a gallon of gas.
Orion: A common Irish surname.
Pavo: Drooling on command, but without the love.
Pegasus: A Christian board game.
Pictor: A large machine designed to harvest grains of rice.
Puppis: Born in a litter.
Pyxis: Straws filled with colorful sugar.
Reticulum: An undesirable form of cancer.

Sagitta: The perpendicular distance h from an arc's midpoint to the chord across it.
Sculptor: Robert Smithson was one of my favorites.
Scutum: Part of the male genitalia, containing two aries.
Serpens: Snakes, duh.
Taurus: The bestselling mid-sized sedan, five years in a row!
Telescopium: A naturally occurring mouthwash that expands & contracts.
Triangulum: Skyping with two other people.
Ursa Major: A bad fit for Goldilocks.
Vela: The fluffy side of Velcro.
Volans: Just turned five years old.
Vulpecula: A man who stimulates a woman's outer genitals with his chest.

Chad Davidson

SILLY

So that when my mother fell down the steps
of our deck on our street named for some dead
president few remember now, I remembered, yes,
this Georgia spring, we're alive, like the dogwoods,
which exploded in cheap party favors of white
bright enough you could read by them, something
by Faulkner maybe, or, if you were just not up for it,
some picture book on dinosaurs whose bones
we still dig up mostly in the West under all
that rock, those vast sunsets, technicolor orange
like the fruit pulp globbed in a sangria pitcher
left over on the deck, one side still beaded, tinted
rose, that night, when my mother fell down the steps,
while I was amazed at the dogwoods again, all hype
and silly, which, my mother couldn't tell you,
originally meant *blessed, touched*. All the while,
the tiny cosmologies of purples and blues
discovered her calves, her ankles, because what was
the interior world of the spirit to the Anglo-Saxons
has become, through cosmic spite or just plain laziness,
exterior, bodily, and, so, *silly*, the way I behaved
in front of my mother, silly to laugh at my own reflection,
when I know, I swear, I saw it coming all along.

Travis Denton

TO A (BUICK) SKYLARK

> *Teach me half the gladness*
> *That thy brain must know,*
> *Such harmonious madness*
> *From my lips would flow*
> *The world should listen then,*
> *as I am listening now!*
>   —Percy Bysshe Shelley

Crooning in the driveway with your thirty-five year old grin,
idling over the miles you've driven to make it to my door,
do you remember driving I-40 all night, hammer down,
ghost towns clicking off the map like daisy petals fall in spring rain,
engine humming, drinking gasoline like sailors slam shots of gin?
Do you often think of those nights at some frosty Lover's Lane,
windows fogged as you rocked on your axles? Did you wish then,
you could stay until morning, waiting for the sun to palm
    the rusty sandstone
scattered around you? How many times did you wish
you could set pen to page and send postcards home,
snapshots recording a purple sun dipping behind the Sandias,
water rushing through the hot springs at Jemez,
or simply how the broken white lines urged you on another mile,
a tether pulling you to Vegas, or on to L. A.
or back South, your home—dear God, if only there was something
you left there, something to get back or reconcile?
And when you saw, as you must have, buzzards spiraling
down just off the roadside, did they remind you, as they often do me,
of dying? Did you imagine your golden skin flaking in the sun,
or those tired mornings to come when you just can't move an inch,
only groan and sputter—those days like today when breath
is frozen smoke with someone like me cheering you on,
sitting with you, an aged wreck refusing consolation
like a bad child, overtired, wanting nothing more than to be left alone.

Melissa Dickson

TAKING THE BACKROADS TO THE ORTHODONTIST

My son explains how a *Three Musketeers* is like bauxite
        which he says is expensive to mine and a nonrenewable resource
but has holes in it like the candy bar he has to write
        about using at least one analogy or metaphor. "Like bauxite,"
he says, with an outside "slick as clay, the color of mud."
        I draw a cloud in the dashboard dust hoping to suggest
the nougat center is fluffy like a cloud, a simile
        I think his teacher will appreciate, but he says, "Nice geode."
So I draw a sun and point out the window where there
        are no clouds after all. He says, "Mars is a dead planet
but full of iron—that's why it's red." And I wonder
        if he knows that the *Three Musketeers* bar he ate
last night, because a boy with braces can't have a *Milky Way*
        is made by the Mars company which also makes
the *Milky Way*. I wonder if he knows how much nougat
        looks like bauxite with its sediment of almonds
and pistachios. Though the *Three Musketeers* nougat
        is nothing like that, just whipped chocolate with holes,
like he said. "Mom?" he asks as we wind toward Dr. Cranford's
        where new wires will be tightened against his teeth
already clad in stainless steel, "Do you understand
        what I mean by Aluminum Ore?" I don't, but I can see
his assignment coming together: the candy bar, the planet
        with its frozen core orbiting just beyond ours, the miners
in Les Baux scratching at the countryside's open sore
        for nearly 200 years, the nonrenewable resource unbound
from its wrapper—"It's like a book you can't judge
        by its cover," he says. Like Alexandre Dumas, his face
as plump as a geode, his hair like whipped meringue.

Michael Diebert

LETTER TO FERRIS FROM DECATUR

Good Jim: A rare fog this a.m. The backlit trees guard their secrets.
Single leaves dangle from branches like Christmas ornaments.
Our friend Hopkins had it right—the world is charged. I don't want
to write another word about not being able to write. Toledo
treats you well, I trust. Is life still full? I'm still doing the work
I was meant to do, still brushing the scales from my students' eyes.
Egg is to yolk as work is to disappointment. When I take care
to remember that, I enjoy myself. Of course I enjoy myself
more when I can sit here, watch the vapor from my coffee,
look out the window, and read meaning into the rain-sheen
on the deck. Me and my little poems. Pain is hard to do
justice to. One of many reasons I am in awe of you. Re politics,
I live on a blue island in a sea of red. Progressive. Cozy.
The school system, though, is a revolving door of corruption.
Give me a beer on the patio at one of our lovely pubs: that's policy
I can get behind. Let's see. Our last meeting was in Chicago,
the Evergreen, that dyed-in-the-wool old-school Chinese joint
beneath the concrete moan of the Stevenson. It was cold.
I remember zip about the food. We were tired, enervated
from two days of full immersion in the river of words,
words, and more words. Scrape of silverware, passing of platters.
You recommended a book which I later read and quite enjoyed.
We were talking about fame. That conference can be an ego-
stroke or -blow. Or both. "Thank God for anonymity," you said.
I nodded heartily and resumed looking at my plate.
I've met myself a lot in my life. Do we live in Venn diagrams?
There I go again. I need to be Bukowski-loud, Ginsberg-garrulous.
But the world is also charged with silent, eloquent gestures:
our server's tiny, embarrassed smile, the iridescent fish
going nowhere, cutting clean angles in the humming, bubbling water.
The fish tank of language. Jim, I wish to swim with that much purpose.
We ate until we were sated. We paid the bill. We walked back
across Wentworth to your car, got in, drove to the reading,
and sat respectfully in the back. This is the world. Anonymity:
I hear you, but I have to think on it. Keep life full. All best, Michael.

Maudelle Driskell

ELEGY FOR THE BOY I NEVER WAS

The men lit the fires in the corners of the field. When Rob was old enough,
they gave him a can and a torch and set him to burning. It starts like this,

the division. Labor. Knowledge. Scars and calluses. The post between
Grandfather and Father, beers, and fire. Soot-gilded faces

alchemic in red light. But Rob dangled his legs from the tailgate,
holding an Old Milwaukee he would not drink—

Nor when it was done would he walk the field
passing the animals as black as the ground,

twisted among the burnt stubble as in the stories he heard
them tell, stories of war:

Animals thin enough won't burn.
Flames starve on their bodies.

Rob makes his family and life with other men:
they have the licenses to all the secrets.

Now, only the women are left to burn the fields.
And we don't know why the coyotes have come back.

Our dogs take up with them and hunt, mate, probably die.
The old yellow bitch stares at the woods, listening

to the pack, the barks, the howls.
She trembles and strains, pacing the edge

of the cleared land. But she won't go to them:
we are the ones who feed her.

Blanche Farley

MASON'S BRIDGE

Because memory is fickle, it is not the bridge
   I remember, or the picnic place itself,
      exactly, but the broad back of the man
         springing down to mottled waters.

Only later could I fathom the danger –
   his little daughter having jumped, fully clothed
      from the crude diving-board,
         unable to swim.

Her frilly white skirt
   must have fluttered a moment
      above the brown pond,
         her thin legs pumping.

She must have felt safe by the sheltering oaks,
   her family near – this girl, my age,
      just five or six, and giddy
         with the Fourth of July.

Maybe she plunged while I fingered the melons
   that cooled near the shore. I don't know.
      Her name, her face, her struggling cries
         have flown.

I recall no sound
   the rescuer made as he split the dark surface.
      Just his strong back, arched in memory, holds.
         It spans the gap between the saved
            and drowned.

LAUGHTER

Our grandfather owned a Victrola
and a few thick records that he liked to play
summer evenings on the farmhouse porch.
Think of it – the way the children sat cross-legged
on the wide wood floor, our grandmother

dashing out the screen door,
untying her apron as the sharecroppers came.
Eight or ten of them. Black faces, white ones,
the workday's dust still in their hair.
They would stand in the yard, my mother says,
as long as the records turned,
the same songs every time.

No one complained. (Perhaps they smelled
the scuppernongs in the arbor, or Grandmother's
sweet shrubs in the yard, depending
on the season.) At last, "the laughing record" played –
played loud and lusty on the edge of darkness.

It was nothing more than a man laughing,
laughing on and on, till the notion caught
and everyone in earshot laughed hard with him.

Elizabeth Fields

WISHING ON A STAR

I want my hair to be as big
as an ol' Cadillac. Curls to crawl

between the cracks like vines
to climb across rear views

splayed up and twinin' out country
roads n twistin' through my toes.

I want my hair to swing all free
like Wisteria in the trees

curls flouting good ol' Southern roots
won't be described as weeds.

I want my curls big enough
to reach down 85, Pines 'n

Magnolias gonna hunker
when my hair drives by.

And when my curls grow
humid large in the thick Georgia

breeze they'll saunter down to
Savannah town and tumble out to sea.

Rupert Fike

BACON GREASE

We used it every day, never got sick –
a scooped glob into the iron skillet
for fried grits, grilled cheese, anything really,
its jar on the stove a vertical Rothko,
top creamy layers melding first
to ochres then a burnt speckled brown,
the mysterious pre-Cambrian band
we never got to since there was always
a new pour-off from each morning's bacon,
a father's job, two hands on the handle,
two tendons rising off his forearm,
today's hot fat dissolving yesterday's
but not for long. By lunch the bubbling
had reverted to its stasis of gel,
an arterial caution we never heeded
because this was my great aunt's kitchen,
under her protection, this was the place
where things were kept as they always were.

And once the pan was hot, the grease crackling,
raw chicken was touched with hands that then touched
whatever they wanted – fridge door handles,
mouths, knives in flaking lead-paint drawers.
Under the sink an open rat poison box,
its skull and crossbones so very normal.
Rare pork chops for dinner, thermometers
broken to retrieve the toy of quicksilver,
mercury rolled from one child's palm to the next.
Smoke trails from both parents' Camels at dinner,
summer's rotating fan always cageless,
its cord frayed at the overloaded plug,
pennies in the fuse box, metal garbage can
bottoms writhing with afternoon maggots,
my great aunt drawing the line at that one,
prescribing a pour of bleach then hot water.
That was my job – kill all those baby flies.

Ann Fisher-Wirth

SUNDOWN, SAVANNAH

She came through the door
while I stood at the stove carefully shaking cayenne

into the chicken noodle soup, and there she was
in her white nightgown. *Mama* I said,

it is you, your own face and body—
and she grinned at me as she never grinned in life.

Cicadas whirred in the privet. A bullfrog plunked
the opening notes of summer. The final bits of sunlight

like a jointed delicate spider
glimmered through the melancholy trees.

I said, *I will give you anything you want, I will
do anything for you because here you are.*

Just let me be near you, she replied. So I turned
from the stove and led her into the little green bedroom

where, propped on pillows, she could watch me
like a child as I moved about the kitchen.

As I pulled the quilt up, her warm, imperceptible hand
began to stroke my cheek. *It's all right, it's all right.*

Gregory Fraser

AGAINST FORGETTING SMALL TOWNS

Thunder's empty promises
through nights of drought, heat
lightning slashing the fields;
streets crisscrossed like kindling
that wished to catch; backs of farm
hands mapped to nowhere.
And star-fields beheld midday
in barns with roofs in rot; and photos
in "salons" of high-school belles—
smooth, untouchable,
lonely as marble nobles
in villas no one cared to fathom
or pronounce—girls winter-eyed
behind the spring. And boys
on corners spitting cocksure
terms, shells of sunflower seeds.
(What an approach to learning,
this.) Now take that boyhood by
the scruff, lead it to the kitchen
sink, apologize to mother, stuck
always with your chores. Take
the millpond brown and humming
to itself, an Old World tinker,
kin to largely German stock.
And the piece inside you, friend?
Do not say it fades like a long
fly ball absorbed by sun
or floodlights of a summer
dusk, when Georgia gathered
after supper with cans of beer,
spiked iced tea on bleachers,
to cheer for kids it bore, kids
it was, and kids it goes on trying
to recall in the same small town—
the town itself (its firehouse,
grocery, library of a few good
books) drifting now over the left
field fence, into high, unsearchable
weeds, if you allow. Do not.

Alice Friman

RED CAMELLIA

The bush has reaped her reward:
she cannot hold up her arms. A salute
to her location at the corner of the house
where the sun is beguiled to stop all day,
and the wasp tending its cells under
the shed roof swoons at the riot of red
multiplying in its compound eyes.

March has finally given way,
and spring in Georgia, primed
with lascivious plumpings,
has sent word: we've little time.
The camellia has waited all year
locked in her thin verticals
for the sun's first hot speech.
Now she answers—one voice
blowing from two-hundred mouths.

Love, I want to talk camellia talk,
quick, before summer's endless
conscription in a green uniform—
that stifling march into fall.
Speak to me. Be my sun, my day star.
Look into my eyes until I'm lost to sight,
then juice me up red and barbarous:
a phalanx of redcoats, a four-alarm fire.
I'm tired of pork roasts and ease
in an easy chair. Bring me one more
season. A reason. Bring it in your hands.

Lee Furey

GOING BACK TO THE RIVER

The night she died I slept through a storm
on a sandbank in the river where I was born.
The tent had blown over twice
with me inside it as I tried to set it up.
Outside my husband led the drunken paddlers
intent on raising only their half-assed song to Ruby.
I felt sand between my grinding teeth
and fell asleep angry, right at home.
The woods the river ran through had been
wrecked by floods the year before,
the week I'd come back and left at once
to swim in an underwater world
where everything made more sense.
Mama told me then it was my Saturn return:
the child-eater, the law-giver,
the planet of tasks and obligations.
Between honeymoon dives and fights
we watched the flood on CNN;
her words turned over and over in my mind.
I sat on the manufactured beach one night
drinking countless shots of the local rum,
deciding it was too late for annulment,
entertaining the Colombian waiter, who said,
"excuse me, mees – are jou from Texas?"
and found it funny every time.
I ordered another and waved him away
to let me watch the ocean-blooms in peace.
A foolish child, I had imagined, I saw,
that all the old problems would be gone,
that I had defeated the monsters
with age and education.
But they had grown up, too,
silent and invisible at my side.
In the Flint the water ran silty,
the landscape pitiful and beaten,
the church of the oaks
changed to ripples and snags in the current.
The old river, its glory and danger wound
through so many of my dreams,
gone, just that easy.

Elizabeth Garcia

LABOR DAY, ONE YEAR MARRIED

The day we carted river rock from front yard
to back, I was thinking of Courbet's *Stonebreakers*,
its muted blues and grays washed out

against the bright, and you knew the sun
was beating on their backs—on ours,
each shovelful hunched over, clouds of dust

escaping rock bodies like souls.
I shoveled into a mesh wastebasket,
hoping it would sift the dirt, then buckled

over its fullness to rattle out the pebbles
into wheelbarrow. My husband
shoveled directly there, and when its apron filled,

carted to the back, wobbling drunk under the weight.
I don't know how many shovelfuls I'd strained against, committed,
before noticing the quiet that had settled on my shoulders

for some time. That stopping, I knew he was back there, sitting.
Breathing. Hiding how the weight he'd added on
was bearing down on him, lungs filling with the rocks,

shovel by shovel, wishing he'd spent that extra hundred bucks
for someone else to do this, thinking that one year ago,
we were young, and no one minded all that rock.

Sarah Gordon

APERTURES: ANDALUSIA
For Flannery O'Connor

Each day the eye finds fresh fare,
filling the homely bowl
of routine with slivers of light
and shade so that even the cracks
in the plaster are crooked roads
to somewhere:
A car shudders up
the dusty drive, cadenced
voices pass the time of day
in the familiar dance,
gauging their moves, a bow,
a do-si-do around the corners
of the room, as glasses perspire
onto the tabletop, a door shuts.
A boy or a man or just a figure
in the distance climbs
onto the sloping back
of a mule. Somebody brings
news that won't wait the telling,
that doesn't bear repeating
but will be repeated,
somebody's mouth a long O,
agape, *agape*, a love feast.
The bloody sun burns low
enough to set the woods on fire,
one arm grazes another
that doesn't want to be touched.
A plate of slightly rotting fruit
rests on the dining room table,
ink-smeared fingers endlessly
turn the pages of the newspaper
or carefully place the rosary
in the bureau drawer.
A former tenant visits,
he doesn't want to leave,
he stands for a long time

in the middle of the yard
running his fingers through
his greasy hair, clearing
his throat, repeating himself.
The tops of trees are silvered
by an antique light.
For a moment a peafowl
stands on one leg
on the roof of the barn,
a live weather vane,
another fans himself
in the front yard.
Nobody notices.
A window slams shut.
The hired man's children
in the back of the car
swat each other with comic books.
Is that smoke on the horizon,
do you smell it, no, well then.
A meal is served, nobody speaks.
Outside, it's early evening,
the bats lilt through the air
as though they are beautiful.
They are small black doors
into the dark.

Robert Gray

WHEN SKIES ARE GREY

we wish our lives awash in sunlight
believing the beautiful days
are clear skied and fair yet i
driving home in intermittent rain
behold this scene
the world around me
bathed in the spirit of warm
black storm clouds
luminously sublimely ominous

for this north georgia landscape
normally bland in late winter
is painted in a fluorescent beauty
colors more vivid
contrasts more defined
especially the greens
the incremental nascent greens
of coming spring

i've noticed this too
in michigan in early may
with the tulips and maturing leaves
but here in late february
with the dull prosaic
greys and browns of
naked hardwoods
the greys and yellows of
hay and dormant kudzu
creating contrasts with the evergreens
and greening grass

and i remember rilke
how beauty is as close
to terror as we can possibly endure

you must feel to live

Beth Gylys

WINTER TO SPRING

Each year the dull colors
seep into you like the sound
of a sigh. You awaken
heavy; you go to sleep heavy.
The drenched, glaucous
heft of the sky squats
on your happy like a stuck pig.
Sickly, plucked, you manage,
with great effort, to stand,
to eat, to move through days
as if through coagulate slop.

Finally, the sun's pistons
start to fire again—you feel
yourself unspooling—something
inside you is breaking apart.

Then, one day, like a switch
flicked to light up the stage—
presto!—outside a flurry of bird
and blossom, buzz and whiff, each
smell tugging your nose a different
direction, and color everywhere:
lavender, periwinkle, chiffon, chartreuse…
every angle a suffusion, spores of pollen
thickening the air until the whole world
is slightly out of focus, and the word
alive hardly seems a place to start.

NARCISSUS

In clusters, the slender,
girlish stems thrust
almond-shaped tips
up through the dirt,
while tentacle legs
lower unseen into banks,
along ridges, in rows
at the edges of yards.

Soon, sun-glazed
or etched by the cool
droplets that they later
drink through their feet
like a party trick,
their minds explode
into electric gold
show-stoppers, coronas,
fanned by the six,
silk-soft perianth.

Mornings their pale
diaphanous faces
lean toward the burn,
and you cup them
with your fingers,
thinking, *Who wouldn't
bend before the water
to worship this?*

D.L. Hall

SILENCES

The letter my father never sent says he is sorry
        he didn't buy me the white rabbit
fur in Jackson, Wyoming or the silver peace ring
        in Juarez, Mexico on vacation in 1975.

He pens apologies for not recognizing the needs
        of his 12-year-old girl who spoke
the language of skin and grew mute without
        her talismans, star-gazing in silence.

I keep thinking about the absence of words, empty
        rooms where thoughts dance like ghost
girls too shy to glance up. How they ride home alone
        in a carriage, down a luminous shell rock

road while a tunnel of night closes in. How late news
        shows up drunk at my door, carelessly
mixing words like *dead, 4 months ago, Mike*
        and the rise of the gag, the lump of never-again

turning into an absence without name. I think of how
        John Lennon penned words reassuring a young
musician in 1977. Intercepted, the letter sold at auction
        and found its way 34 years later to the intended.

I think of how Lennon's ink-thin and brittle words breathe
        a late bond from the no-longer-living,
how the last time I saw Mike, I was punishing
        him with my silence. My last act,

a blank gulf. When our eyes locked, he watched me pass,
        his lips mouthing words to a clerk. My gait,
pulling me; my blink was the final clip ending twenty years
        of knotted back & forth.

Maybe I'm the ghost girl too shy to speak–a lost girl
        looking for talismans. In the carriage, I strain
toward a morning where I'm wearing silver rings and rabbit
        fur, penning words, mailing letters, shouting names.

Derrick Harriell

MAGIC CITY

You stole the universe unseen
the universe pretty complicated
constellations and slid them South/
didn't you/ Atlanta/
you crackled sequined bang loud
it felt hush silent against
hush reticent/ those eyes
leaning out faces/ a field of archivists
tell future grandchildren eyes
back in my day we jumped/
we jumped the fuck out faces
and died on a stage in Magic City
and didn't give a fuck/
didn't they/ Atlanta/
You bleeding a green ceiling
caping untainted pretty/
all this untainted pirouetting
above us/ no one sees or sings
guns/ all these guns poking
waists like stripper stings/
no one sees or sings
Hennessy/ all this Hennessy
ride us drunk like jockeys/
and all we want are women
and record deals/ Atlanta/
coffin loads of women
and record deals

Pamela Hart

RIVER OF PAINTED ROCKS

Along the Chattahoochee we walk. Men fish in its muddy shoals. Also cormorants. Pelicans. I'm proud. It's the marching. The uniform. The order. Heat oozes. Fish break the cinnamon surface. I notice your eyelashes. How dark. You were a blond baby. Now you are a dark soldier. You have an Adam's apple I see. Your skin is clear. I hear my father saying your skin is clear. I talk to him for a very long time in the parking lot of the Red Barn Restaurant. It's our last lunch. I don't know this then. See how the mind is torn from topic to topic. We don't visit Carson McCullers' house. She married a soldier from Fort Benning. Its stucco houses, the red-tiled roofs. You liked to paint. You were not an artist. There's no rushing mountain stream to this story.

William Ogden Haynes

HOMECOMING

The Greyhound dropped me
about a mile back on Georgia State Route 50
because they don't travel these county roads.
It was about another two miles
until I reached the long dirt and gravel driveway
leading to my family home.
About a quarter mile down the drive
sat a white Victorian Greek Revival with pillars
and a large shaded front porch.
But even from that distance
I could tell it was Bessie,
our long-time maid
who raised me,
running toward me
leaving a trail of dust
between the grand boulevard of oaks.
It was as if she was running in slow motion,
but as she got closer I could see her smile
and the tears on her cheeks.
Then this sixty year old daughter of slaves,
said *welcome home Mr. Johnny*
and jumped into my arms
making me drop my suitcase
to catch her.
I'll always wonder why my mother,
like a lavender rose pressed in a book,
stayed up on the front porch in a rocking chair,
sipping her iced tea
on the day I returned home
from the great war.

M. Ayodele Heath

FATHER TO SON, OR A BRIEF HISTORY OF OKRA (MASTER'S TAKE)

Discovered in her wild state
on the flood-plain of the Nile,
Okra arrived at Port of New Orleans
circa 1700:
Germs stored in a drum.

Start Okra from seed. She does not transplant
well. She's best planted
in Southern soil, after all danger
of frost has passed.

RULE OF THUMB: Keep them
separated. Okra seeds are large, easy
to handle, but they need
warm weather to grow well.

In Northern climes, you won't have
much of a crop.

Picking pods while wet
may darken their skin which
might make them seem bitter
at first. But really, their taste
is unaffected.

Unlike her fairer cousin, Cotton,
Okra's showy yellow flower
blooms just one day a year:

Just make sure that day don't last
too long.

Graham Hillard

WATCHING DAYBREAK ON THE SAVANNAH

One hundred miles south and east,
Oglethorpe and Tomochichi bartered for use
of the river. Here the earth is host
to more recent dead, bones
bound by a whisper of tissue
but bound still, deposited and left for
the rending of their parts to dust.
The ground hasn't recovered yet
from their intrusion. It buckles and swells,
its grass sparse and pale even at the height
of spring, untended since the dissolution
of the church that stood here once, kept
the stones and the memories of the dead. Now,
weeds touch the names themselves and may cover
this place one day if left to. Mosquitoes breed
amidst the vagueness of the holy. I come here
to acknowledge something I don't know,
to pay a tribute to what holds, what
lives alongside the longleaf
pines, the spiral ladies-tress sprung
from a grave, feeding. A sunrise odor
chokes this morning: wet hair, bleach cut
to the smallest factor. The fog
that should have held like a transparent skin
to the river peels instead away.
The water is raw beneath it.

Laurence Holden

WHAT'S NEEDED

What's needed
is water
and dark

moving to a time
as slow as roots

in a well

where silvered fish
swim

in a dream
of knowing

not caught
but foreseen.

Karen Paul Holmes

POEM THAT BEGINS WITH A DEFINITION

A passive sentence is often composed by a passive
person. It is written with a subject acted upon
by a verb, sort of like being assaulted.
A phantom subject is preferred by governments,

corporations and scientists: *Written complaints*
will be read and answered in three days.
It has been decided you are not eligible for benefits.
The solution was heated to boiling.

This idea was thought up by someone anonymous.
The similes were excavated one by one,
like grapefruit triangles with a serrated spoon.
Then, edits were marked by a red pencil.

This poem will be appreciated by people
who don't like action or responsibility.
This poem will be satisfying to few
because its conclusion was eaten by the dog.

H. Holt

COILS OF WHITE

coils of white
surround the south,
where sundry scandals
on slave-lorn fields
vexed freedom's silver
with pointed hoods;

time's passage pours
marble dust in mouths
aiming to damper rage
and remove tasteless,
unmitigated bigotry
while the jaundiced,
mellow moon judges
the Judds "old days"
as fools' scripture

straight snips seek
to change this fault,
though gold is hard
to come by

Peter Huggins

WOODPECKER

A woodpecker shimmies
Up my house, pecking holes
In the cedar siding.

I gather stones
The Chattahoochee
Made smooth and clean.

I miss the woodpecker,
Hit the side of my house,
Release a swarm of bees,

Run inside.
The woodpecker flies away.
The bees return to their hive,

The stones to the garden.
I repair the cedar with PVC board.
I bring my life into balance.

Sara Hughes

WHAT YOU MUST UNDERSTAND

When my father hit me, he hit out of love.
His own father taught him to give
as good as he got, but he gave pain
only when he had no other choice.
Sunday mornings, helping him shave,
I pumped a marshmallow glob of foam
in his palm. He smeared the cream
over his blonde stubble, rinsed his hand,
began. The razor, like a finch, swooped
from ear to chin, plunged through air,
battered the sink water. The naked blade
rose and raked his jaw. He never spoke
during this ritual of erasing.
He hummed hymns. I sat on the edge
of the tub, looking up to him. He winked
at me in the mirror, whacked the razor,
and scraped his young throat clean.
When he finished, I snapped
a wet washcloth across his bald skin
and slapped Old Spice on his cheeks.
See, my father didn't scare me.
I was a little girl who wanted nothing
but a father who told the truth.
I believed him every time he said
This hurts me more than it hurts you
as he pulled the belt from his pants.

T.R. Hummer

SLOW TRAIN THOUGH GEORGIA

The mist that rises from this river solidifies the air
Underneath the rusty trestle where a train has come and gone.
It is the precipitate of the chemical morning, dumped
Unceremoniously into the clear solution of a summer night.
Hours earlier, the midnight freight detonated under starlight
Three hours late and thundering toward Birmingham, the red glow
Of the steel mills, the tincture of that constant dawn.
But now the air shuts down. Now the distant whistles of the morning shift
Into the throats of mockingbirds, and the sun works
Its electrolytic clarity from the top down, starting with the ozone.
The mist rising off the muddy little river curves south beyond the bridge.
It follows the water, of which you might be tempted to imagine
It is the astral body, downstream toward the Gulf –
Because you want to believe in the soul of the river, don't you,
You want a name and a positive destination
For this ghostly swath like a scar between banks of new-leafed oaks,
As if the world had a center and you were standing in it,
As if everything turning were your own self-evident revolution.
But watch this scene long enough and the sun
Will defeat you, the beautiful obscurity of the mist
Will dilute and disappear. Already the revelation is working
Its inevitable way toward you from the upper atmosphere. Soon
The oil-scummed image of the surface of the river will superimpose
Its visionary dreariness on what you can see of the earth:
Red clay, a distant cotton field, the tin roof of a tenant house
Where morning touches a mirror and moves at the constant speed of light
To touch the face of the sleeping man who stirs and touches his wife
Who is awake already, worrying over breakfast, remembering
The deep-night noise of the train that stopped
Whatever dream she might have had, the double blackness
Of coal-heaped gondolas hours after midnight, the anonymous steel
Of wheels against greased rails, inhuman, turning – like everything she knows
About God and politics – against her, going nowhere.

Jamie Iredell

CHATTAHOOCHEE LOW TIDE

Tonight the moon is new, dark as a continent,
but plump enough to play the earth with tides,
to pluck the strings of your body, curvy as a guitar.
Its tidal tug as the blood rushes
to our most tender parts, where heat meets skin,
like landing on a virgin shore where the natives
await in poppy fields, roasted pig meat
steaming on platters held high overhead.
And the moon has pulled the water to another
hemisphere, and the pools expose moccasin nests,
wisteria roots—their tentacles tendriling the oaks.
And the mussels and trout crowd upon each other.
And out beyond the launch in the river's low tide chasm
the otters feed, as I feed on you, here where we want
to be, our fists pounding against the dock.

Robert Perry Ivey

TO HOME

Head south on Old Highway 41
until the dead white oak with burnt limbs
half raised like Black Preacherman praying.

You know you're going right
when you see bullet holes in a weight limit sign
and busted bottles at its base

beside a river rock chimney
standing in the woods, houseless,
like the last tombstone in an overgrown graveyard.

Then turn east on the dirt road
with a pollen covered pond
yellow from pine paint spilt all over it.

Now take care over Flat Bridge.
There ain't many creek crossings
made of wood no more.

Just past rusted car yards
and piles of tar baby railroad ties
you'll smell the city of forsythia blooms.

And further South, at the end
of Spur 19, in the cherry blossom's shadow,
Macon, the heart of Georgia.

This is where Walking Man pulls pins off pine cones
and heaves them at cars in a long arm arc
like he's still on ambush.

This is where Sammy Legs the Bum
wallows his fist around in his armpit
and picks wasp nests off your stoop for 5 dollars,

where the Ocmulgee River runs red
by a hilly cemetery lined with roses
and crypts rise and yawn when the water's up.
This is where I will lay my bones down.

Mike James

TALKING WITH ALLEN GINSBERG, IN A DREAM
for John Stephens

i'm in ginsberg's apartment
he sips tea
from a ceramic cup with no handle
looks thoughtful in a white, cotton kimono
that's a little stained, a little frayed at sleeves
the kimono's half open
shows gray hairs above a
wrinkled, pot belly
as he leans against his small kitchen counter
not a "cooker's kitchen"
instead a place to heat canned soup
make sandwiches
eat late night yogurt and veggie snacks

i tell him
my favorite of your books
is the last one
death and fame

you like posthumous things
he asks
cause i do…always have…even now

i tell him
it's mainly that last poem
the one about your funeral
i love those
jokey lines

i'll show you how i do it
he says
(starts to sway back and forth)
begin slowly or quickly
clear your mind
let one thought bleed to another
this can take a while

maybe an hour or twelve
that last poem was good
could have been bad
too often are
that's ok
turn bad poems into paper airplanes
bless them and toss

Gordon Johnston

CANOE

She begins and ends, comes and goes, in confluence,
her bow and stern a merging of gunwhales, arrow-ends of a boat-long
bending. To kneel within her is to be notched on the current's taut line.

She is less a weapon to cut water than a soft answer said to it – a *yes* spoken
to this sentence or that of the river's shifting sermon. Midship, like the current
that rolls her on, she widens, her bottom, like the riverbed, an oxbow.

She is ordinal and original, quick and dead, ending as she began
in the shape of a wave, a curl in air whose outer edge, followed,
becomes the rounded keel, trued to the river's wide will.

Filled by a falls, she would still float, limning the green skin of the water –
of the river, in her, yet still all herself, knowing as she is known—emptied of me.
Going on.

Melanie Jordan

APOCALYPSE TACKLEBOX

rubberbanded dollars oily
from recounting. A green face
folded in half.

two tampons like lures,
eyeless.

a confetti of pills

(a gap in a smile, nothing
useful fits here)

triple A batteries cribbed
from latchkey tv

(972) 386-4577; the one
I45 motel unbooked
an hour ago

my dumb baby photo
shrunk to fit a fake
gold charm

four Q-Tips;
one Mickey Mouse
Band-Aid

the plastic Green Lantern
ring he put on my finger,
laughing, at the zoo

red Swiss Army Knife
its cargo of sad
stilettos

the sawed-off pencil
dwindling

cut fishing line, my silver
thread to the door where
I entered the labyrinth

black flecks, lint
what might be
lash-like insect legs

two onyx beads,
exiles
never re-strung

a button
missing
its moorings

a needle begging
a miracle
from its eye

Krazy Glue tube
used once
to bind skin and skin

one nail on which
to hang; hang what,
in what house?

a trial lipstick
mistaken
for salve

speckled vitamins
like a world's
magic seed

a spider tucked
all of itself,
a brown knot

old school razorblade
its gray
highway edge

Allen wrench,
hex key

crumbs/sand
Hansel's
atom trail

Andrea Jurjevic

CINÉMA VÉRITÉ: A LOVE STORY

I think I'll eventually forget you,
cross your number, throw keys in the meadow
by the roads you walked, dressed in black and blue.

I'll not think of two bumpkins who hitched to
the cities, left their coastline to erode.
I'm sure I'll forget you, all about you—

every drunken detail, like when you blew
up, sold my records to scrape by. Also,
the roads you walked off, dressed in black and blue.

Like immigrant scum stood in welfare queues,
pawned my mom's gold for daily joints. You rogue,
I'm sure I'll forget you, all about you—

plastic bags, how shitfaced you'd get on glue,
hair like rooks' nests, loafed around the metro
in that jacket I saved for, black and blue.

Even dead scrape the barrel, I assume,
and how foreign words stand out odd, alone.
I swear, I'll forget you, all about you,
how you bled on tracks, dressed in black and blue.

BLACKBIRDS
After Wallace Stevens

the only thing moving
in the city
in front of the cars' silver headlights

is the man on the bicycle

the day too young
still too damp
for shadows

the man and the black bicycle
slink across the zebra
as one

this handsome diligence on thin wheels
their spinning irises
and his feet
like two blackbirds

in steady flight

one follows the other
edging the circle
they make

and in their fixed rhythm
their closeness
and the distance between them
remains the same

a sweet pursuit
now clearing into the park
in the cool whirl of the wind
and then the empty path

and the city silent in their departure

the day was young and pale all week
it was silver
and it was going to rain feather

Lissa Kiernan

ATOMS FOR PEACE

> *On February 16, 2010, U.S. President Barack Obama announced $8 billion in federal loan guarantees to build two nuclear reactors in Georgia, three decades after the Three Mile Island nuclear accident halted all new reactor orders.*

Five hours into jury pool, I am burned out
on poetry. What am I thirsty for?
News—good news.

MSNBC, guide me through
this inverted world, turned back
180 degrees on its stalk.

Enough of this crazy heat!
I feel impelled to speak today
in a language that in a sense is new.

I, too, would like a plan for clean,
safe energy. One which generates
jobs ideally, since I am now six

paychecks behind. One that fills
in the pit of partisanship
with some sensible, recyclable waste.

Voir dire. To see them say. False
etymology. I see the President say it.
His lips, that is, are moving.

But how do I know that he believes,
with every atom, his axiom?
Whether he's seen the burning

bush, the worried wind, the patient sun?
Just one. Who stands light-rinsed
for the camera with the clarity of a star.

Anna King

LIKE LINEN ON THE CREPE MYRTLE

He and I did end years before when groceries were good enough to call it quits. Letting go again is the whisper of a ravaged urn. A shiver stolen from the hemline of winter is why I could not forgive him. I have no idea what to do with this emptiness again other than spinweavegather it all into a star filled cloak. The salted August and the fevered October are erased from odd numbered pages of magazines I recycle. A bruise colored sunrise was like linen on the crepe myrtle. The crepe myrtle was a beautiful thing I touched like our child in the sea.

Bill King

WINTER SONG

after W.S. Merwin

I miss the spring peeper
who crawled out
the rain fed pond
all summer
until every one
green and wood frogs too
buried themselves in mud
beneath ice or snow

and I miss the first big rain
that made little throats
trill from bent stems
of elderberry and curly willow
from green leaves of young maple
that shade the street
behind the grocer
that faces state route 33
and the rest of the world

all of this has gone now
unfleshed except for sky
scarred with jet trails
going anywhere but here

lover of evening rain
lover of last light
lover of small still water
that gazes at leaves
all summer

come back

Robert S. King

ONE MAN'S PROFIT

The rabbit jerks in ache and panic,
her foot captive in the snare.
The trapper is on his rounds
to check for fur and food.
Long ears fill with dry limbs
cracking under boots closing in.

Sometimes the jaws of fate
demand payment in installments.
As time gnaws, so too the rabbit
quickly chews off her foot
and frees herself from all but pain.
She flees into the shadows
to pay for the rest of her life.

The trapper curses his loss
but pins a chain to the foot,
to be forever linked to the one
who didn't completely get away.
This, he says,
will bring me luck.

Dorothy Knight

THE CLERMONT LOUNGE
Atlanta, GA

They thanked me darling, thanked me love, thanked me honey, when they bent for tips. Blondie licked her top lip and danced in a girdle, told me she kept men in line with her tits. The woman with the bouncing ass said she wouldn't take anything off if nobody tipped, told a groping man she hated white people anyway. The black woman who danced like she wasn't naked in sensible heels held a string of pearls between her cheeks. A man threw a balled up five at her. She called him a motherfucker, asked him if his mama never taught him any manners, threw it back in his white face. The brunette who pop and locked and whose boots skid in a moonwalk paused when the cd skipped, tied her waist length hair in a knot, let it catch on her hips. The blonde with the pistol tattooed holstered said, "Welcome to the gun show," and made her breasts bounce in time to Prince with no hands. The man to my right at the bar told me poetry is dead while a classy trannie dressed as Marilyn Monroe bent wrist and head to take dollar bills from my hands. The landscaper to my left said being here felt like being home between all the high kicks and legs lifts, and Blondie's cans crushing cans for $10 a pop. She cradles her breasts in her hands after and shakes her head at the big bills waving until it doesn't hurt anymore. I bought a $20 lap dance from a 62-year-old blonde named Portia who dresses like little red riding hood and dances to Sam the Sham and the Pharaohs. She smacked her ass and named her grandchildren for me, wagged her finger and told me I couldn't touch before I had tried. She said her feet hurt in her platforms. She asked me if I knew where to find the best peach cobbler in town then pulled aside her nylon panties before I could answer.

It's that rude understanding keeps you coming back, a little beaver with your beer on disco nights at the Clermont Lounge.

Chrissy Kolaya

SAVANNAH

Somewhere in Savannah he's sleeping
in a small room above the garage,
exhaust to wake him in the morning,
fat Labrador curled
at his side. Here's where the au pair slept,
where she came to write letters home, her few
small hours of peace away from the children.

He'll be up with the sun,
out on the golf course with his father
watching an alligator
and its slow amble to the water.
Hard to believe those things can run,
he'll say. Hard to believe anything can
in the kind of heat that hangs over the city.

But he does.
Down the quiet streets,
just the pad pad pad
of his feet on the leaves
that line the gutters.

The children have all gone back to school.
Everyone goes to bed early,
so he goes by himself into town.

Now it's dark,
some bar has a jazz band.
He'll order a beer,
think of an old girlfriend
who phoned to say she's getting married,

will try to remember lying next to her body
wondering if he might have loved her
like that.

Keetje Kuipers

GEORGIA

I've been trying for a year to decide
        if I'm in love with you. Now, red clover
spattered in the ditches, I cross the state
        line on my way to be with you. This week

everything gave itself up to the light,
        dogwood trees and effusive azaleas,
even the dead armadillos, belly
        up to the sun. I still don't know what holds

me back. The sign on the car I pass says
        gone for gas, but that's a lie. Kudzu wound
through the tires, leaves pressed to the glass where
        anyone can see the dust on the dash.

Irene Latham

AT AGE NINETY MY GRANDFATHER NO LONGER GARDENS

No time, he says, as he lifts my grandmother
from her wheelchair to the toilet and back again

spoons rice and cubed JELL-O past unsmiling lips
into her gaping baby-bird mouth

then eases her onto the sofa, careful
to tuck the beaded flannel beneath her chin.

Meanwhile, what was once jubilant rows
of tassled corn and sturdy pole beans

now snarls like a half-starved dog
whose coat is thick with burrs and tangles,

and as my grandmother's breath shuffles in and out
my grandfather dreams of tomatoes:

fat Beefsteak and juicy Better Boys,
Early Girls blushing pink then flaming red,

remembers summers spent weeding and watering,
how he'd palm the tomatoes, give them the slightest twist,

then sit back on his heels as the fruit burst
like fireworks against the back of his teeth.

Joshua Lavender

COMMUNION
At Andalusia

Sprawled in rockers on the screened front porch,
we tell jokes over coffee. A volume of stories,
spine crinkled like laundry before ironing,
lies winged in my lap. I've come in the morning,
broken your routine. In the downstairs parlor
transfigured by bed, Morris chair, and typewriter,
a page clean as new linen curls itself to the scroll.
But you assure me, you don't mind company.
I roll a cigarette, one-handed. Your crutches
stretch like old dogs at your feet. Humming,
I gaze through the screen to where the sun climbs
and a breeze stirs the oaks. "The morning's
so fine," I say, "any time now God may amble
out of the woods or walk up the lane from the gate
and wave at us as He crosses the land." You nod
in your faint way. Two redbirds thrash about
the hedges a while, flutter far down the pasture
to alight in pines. Then, furrowing your brow:
"Or He might not wave at all. And that might be,"
you muse, "a revelation." You clasp your cup
between shaking hands and your voice sinks.
I can't make out the murmured words, only feel
their pulse fleet as gibberish. Or prophecy.

Hank Lazer

N26P49

11/11/13
athens GA

[Handwritten poem arranged in a tree/branching shape:]

sounding it out / in what sense / i hear a / listen up
when is music
sounding board
resonators
from one to another
in f. ogot is in
then what
"he was everything / as / he was speaking about" 1997

Rachel Van Horn Leroy

GEORGIA CYPRESS

Calloused trunk hung with age bent
by an old window. My rings keep ages' chronicles.
My branches hang like Cherokee shawls.
My eyes, brown knotted knobs,
have seen hands working arrowheads
to a point.

Years ago, white men camped by my trunk
and built a white frame house.
Europeans' tense hands fingered guns.
Small blond children played at skirted legs
while husbands cleaned woods.
The white man drove Cherokee away
in a trail of blood and tears.

The pines crashed down.
I knew each one whose body rose into barn roofs.
Sharecroppers toiled in sun; I cast the only shade.
The waving green fields of yield
is where croppers labored through days
and hoed cotton, picked beans,
tobacco, melons, corn, and wheat.

Generations aged my limbs
that shadowed white-shawled women.
Fried chicken popped in cast iron pots
that simmered gravy, greens, and grits.
Bluegrass music rose from banjos,
picking about pipe tobacco.
Settlers became the native tribe,
subdued land once a wilderness.

The old frame house's paint peeled.
The growl of engines came
and brought the hard, gray ground
with dashed lines of yellow paint
that took settlers to the cities.

Alone once again except new sprung trees
my rough aged trunk leans more
as each wide ring emerges in my trunk.

One night the old wood house crashed in.
My leaning trunk creaks like boards
before that sagging house collapsed.
I know one day my trunk
will crash like wooden houses
or old pines that white men severed.
Until that day, I dream of black-haired men
that lived beneath swaying trees.

Kathleen Brewin Lewis

EGGSHELL

The morning is a chiffon scarf. A child
steps out into soft light,
a spotted egg cupped in his hands.
I rest my palm on the place where
his bowed head meets his slim neck.
Sometimes this is prophecy,
sometimes recollection.
To touch him this way is always a blessing.

Afternoon, a chambray shirt, rolls its sleeves up.
The boy lifts his head, tells me
of his dreaming, turns his attention
to the plunge of a red-tailed hawk.
There is composure in his turning.
His shoulders broaden, he grows taller than I.
The egg cracks open. The night is a winter
coat with silver buttons.

John Lowther

AN UNAUTHENTICATED JOHNNY MINOTAUR EPISODE FRAGMENT (TRANSLATED FROM THE CRETAN)

The Emperor Reminisces

Oh that fumbling idiot minotaur (*adorbz*!) bumbling into the trap set for the penultimate President of the United States, James Earl Carter Jr.— *Jimmy, Johnny—Johnny, Jimmy* — he felt the ghost of his glee maneuvering the crowd, his suit (crushed velour), makeup, glued mustache all helping him sweat, but most of all the knowledge: *It's all going down now, my time has come.* He'd cringed when he felt the *glid,* when the lipless one'd whispered, dust voice a bouquet of caramel prunes and dry rot, "Yeass Fritzzz, thiss vill do." then *glid* again and was gone, leaving his cringe to creep his sweaty flesh.

But everything had gone south, gone slant, sunk.

Not the plot of course, Max said it'd be so and S.W.A.S. made it reality in a whirl of delight whose only drawback was the length of time he'd had to pretend to resist. He became the President in short order, the 40th, and then final… from the penultimate peanut farmer to the ultimate Lizard King, the Emperor Walter 'Fritz' Mondale, Exalted Potentate of the Re-United States of America. His first act after being voted Emperor — to ban voting, followed by canceling all debt. That was the rhythm the people liked, you take away something that they pretended to believe was helping them while giving them something they thought it impossible to even want. Imperial Edict numbers 447 (the death penalty for challenges to the Emperor's rule) and 448 (guaranteeing every imperial subject their own reality show with a 3 episode minimum). The one-two punch combo of a S.W.A.S.-based hegemony.

No denying, Max had kept his word, S.W.A.S. had made everything possible— for years he was worshipped by his subjects. That he quickly found ruling tiresome wasn't a problem— S.W.A.S. could handle all that, which he realized is what Max had had in mind all along. The Emperor had enjoyed scrawling "Fritz was here" on nubile breasts, asses, with an arrow pointing to little boy's & girl's assholes (then sending them to be tattoo'd on the Imperial dime), had appreciated all his groupies, his quality intoxicant smorgasbord, and the endless virgins offered up by parents who were… *honored*. Yes, he had enjoyed— but looking back, it was clear too, his main enjoyment had been punishing Johnny. *How many times did I wipe her memory or implant falsies?* he thought, and reminded himself that she was a he back then. If only he'd been able to see *her* sooner, maybe they…

That was the turning point. As long as Johnny was Johnny, a bumbling minotaur— he'd been a perfect fall guy, a most excellent scapegoat. He could still recall fits of uncontrollable giggles at certain headlines— PRESIDENT KILLED BY MINOTAUR DURING BIZARRE NIGHT OF DRUNKEN SEX! POLITICAL ASSASSINATION OR EROTIC-ASPHYXIATION?— Such fun! But only so long as that Minotaur had stayed a Cretan *mister*.

He didn't exactly understand it, but knew he'd caused it. In his desire to find ever-new torments for Johnny, he'd brought about the fall of S.W.A.S., the death of Max, undermined his own rule, and subjected himself to a tyranny more potent than any he'd ever known; *love*. He'd fallen for her, he'd pined, he'd sighed— for Jonni Minotaur. The Emperor couldn't stop feeling it and it distorted his memory of that fateful day— it had been another one-two punch, but personal. He told SWAS to determine Johnny's most profound desire and make it so, planning next to negate it in the most perfectly hilarious/awful fashion...

But by the instantaneous power of S.W.A.S. Johnny became Jonni. Time slowed for the Emperor. Struck down by his own heart, he'd let loose a logico-emotive virus, aka L.A.F.S. within S.W.A.S., which led to Max's beheading up in the satellite, to the earth moving, etc. The earth moving was no metaphor, his Imperial capital, Atlanta— Jewel of the Empire— began to sink (Atlantis à venir). He hadn't realized any of this then, he just stared at Jonni, becoming ever more smitten as he saw her delight at her new body, now poorly appareled in baggy masculine clothes. She'd realized immediately that he'd granted her this, and the look of gratitude, of joy and presence, beamed upon him like a spotlight, like the applause of millions who were not being S.W.A.S.'d into feeling their feelings would have made him feel. She bounded across the room, grabbed his head in both her hands and planted a kiss on his mouth, and then she was dancing for joy around the Imperial bed before racing down the halls of the palace, her happy cries echoing back to him.

Far too late (it was too late instantly too) he realized that something wasn't right with S.W.A.S., citizens were discovering the bio-electric wiring attached to their heads and pulling it out. Once that happened, they began to question having a Dionysian rock star who'd faked his death in a Paris bathtub in 1971 only to re-emerge as an Apollonian Vice President 6 years later, and as their all-powerful Emperor now. That bio-electric writing degraded within hours, its residues in the brain inducing targeted amnesia, which led to more paradoxes in everyday living than a dozen time travel movies generate. By the time he asked S.W.A.S. (having failed to raise Max) what was happening it was no longer able to explain. The only answer it gave was L.A.F.S., it's creaking mechanical voice laughing as it said it. In the lonely lovesick days after he gathered that Johnny's deepest wish had not simply been to be Jonni, but had involved how all others would perceive her and each other, and had invoked the Cretan paradox and others paradoxes too. A series of exponentially ramifying affirmations and deaffirmations had begun to play out throughout S.W.A.S., the "Satellite Crisis" happened and we all watched the news feeds showing Shrek's body strapped into his chair while his head, torn from his neck but still hooked up to that colander-looking thing bounced slowly around in a satellite now spinning. Her desire had only been partially accomplished, before the recursive paradoxes of L.A.F.S. had crashed S.W.A.S. for good. She was she, but her wish for everyone had only partially taken.

There *might* have been a moment when he could've reasserted some kind of control. If so, he missed it— busy as he was, endlessly moping about Jonni, calling her until her voicemail could accept no more, yelling at his Jack Lord to bring Jonni to him and cursing or shooting at him when he failed. & then that idiotic *Max Junior Show* had started up, and *The Johnny Minotaur Show* (starring Kyle Minotaur) got the go ahead for new seasons after having been cancelled by Imperial degree, and what had been his reality for decades became a television fantasy and everyone forgot that they had lived it too. They forgot there had been an Emperor, and all his jello-y minions had stopped coming to work. The ruler of the world's most powerful Empire, Walter Mondale has become simply Fritz, an object of casual scorn.

One of the waiters from The Majestic came outside and yelled at him to stop hassling customers for cigarettes and he cursed, spat and pushed his cart down Cleburne Terrance and parked it by the dumpsters. He spotted a butt, both dry and only half-smoked and snatched it up, sat himself down against the wall in the narrow band of shade and lit up.

The Civil War never ended and the city, Atlanta, continued to sink. But, Jonni, wherever she was— was no longer blinked.

The Minotaur Moves On

Miranda Minotaur (Jonni's stage name) unzipped her skirt and wiggled it passed her hips, letting it fall to the floor. For a moment she stared into the mirror— thankful to be who she was— and her brow scrunchied for a second at the thought of Fritz. She'd spotted him on Ponce down by the Murder Kroger. It wasn't exactly that Jonni had *forgotten*… it was more that she couldn't exactly *remember*, and when she tried, that internal membrane that lets us imagine that real memories are over *here,* and shit we might have just dreamt of, or seen in a movie half asleep and stoned, was over *there*… that membrane was rent with holes. Knowing but not that she knew, she knew without "knowing" that this was why she was knockin' em dead on the stage now. So she kinda didn't want to pick at it. Her lappy *bloop*'d— every last ticket had sold out. Her agent would be after her to extend the run. She scanned the headlines on her latest reviews; "LOVE AT FIRST SIGH" IS A TRIUMPH OF THE SPIRIT; MIRANDA MINOTAUR WILL MAKE YOU LAUGH, CRY AND YES, SIGH! Then her phone rang, but she texted her agent instead, "no 2 ATL, done w this place. time 2 move on. Berlin? Tokyo?" Jonni slipped into some sweats happy not to have to tuck, opened a single serving prosecco and ran a hot bath.

The Immortal Sings

Satellite of Love… Satellite of Love…
"Sat a lite" Max intoned, in time, tunelessly. Unvoiced he also "sang" the descending *bum bum bum* between his *Sat a lite's.* In an actual mood (a novelty for him) he keyed up S.W.A.S.-L.A.F.S. on his mobile device and saw that Fritz had just lit a grimy cigarette butt — a bum had sat to light a

butt— *bum bum bum*— under Max Jr.'s televisually marketable lips Max smiled liplessly (no teeth).

    Next he tapped in a smoothie order (caramel prune with a shot of virgin's blood), headloaded his monologue for the show tonight, and through his proxybot urged Miranda to extend her run in Atlanta, knowing she would refuse. All as expected. The apparent destruction, not just of S.W.A.S., but of the Empire was thoroughly rejuvenating. S.W.A.S.-L.A.F.S. no longer *controlled controllers*, but let their own supposed freedom be their enslavement. There were even people who saw quite clearly that the Civil War was ongoing— they shared infographics, memes, and cellphone videos, but restricted their action to 'likes' and other ineffectual reciprocal narcissisms. Having for years treated love as a mere bit of rhetorical bait, what L.A.F.S. had done to S.W.A.S. was genius in the form of a virus. "Love" was now the carrot and the stick of his infinitely cloaked hegemony. No one who questioned "love" was taken seriously, and indeed, had difficulty taking themselves seriously.

bum bum bum

    Max's smoothie arrived, he glid, he sip'd, he sigh'd

Thomas Lux

FOX

My father said: Fox took another chicken last night
and scared two others to death,
and your goddamn dog never lifted his head.
Kill it. He meant the fox,
not the dog. I followed his tracks
and the small splats
of blood and brown feathers
through the snow (I was glad
it snowed, I couldn't track a moose
on dry ground) to his foxhole
near the top of a steep hill
about a half mile away; fresh, loose
dirt marked it easy among some small pines.
I knew not to go too near
and leave my scent,
so set up a good shot thirty yards away.
I built a small wall of snow, tripodded my rifle.
When he comes out of his den again
I'll shoot the red fox dead.
Two hours later,
I hear my father call: Fox took another chicken!
I moved neither my blue finger
from the trigger nor the crosshairs
off his foxhole. Turns out, he had a back door.
In no foxhole I'd ever seen or heard of—in movies,
comics, TV shows, school, and later, in books,
did a foxhole have a back door; no, only one door,
upward, through the roof—a helmet usually—over which,
and through which, bullets and shrapnel tore.

THE HUNCHBACK FARMHAND

He got that way, said the man who hired him,
by hunching over rows
to do what I hired him to do: hunch over rows,
to twist a stem—beans, squash—and snap it off.
His broken back
bends downward
and to the left. He ate
with us at the picnic table,
leaning on his higher elbow,
after the hay was in,
during which he was little
help: he could lift a bale but not heave it above his hump
onto the flatbed truck.
In a good year, hay's second mowing
is the season's last, so
he'd stay until all the eating was done
and then walked home,
the back way, through the woods,
on a path he knew,
two miles closer
than by road.

Clarence Major

AFTERNOON RAIN

Morning fog lifted. I should be at peace.
High in clay cliff distance: grazing sheep.
At shoreline wild roses and cranberry bogs.
But in this windswept pocket of land I am in deep.

Remains of stress from last week everything fell apart.
I walk to the inlet elbow and sit on a sandy rock.
Choppy waters! Out at sea tiny sails floating like butterflies.
Last week: *airplanes flying into buildings. Thousands dying.*

I pick up a whalebone-fragment.
That same girl with a dog running free!
Noon and as usual it's beginning to cloud over.
Soon rain will come. Clearing by five.
Usual pattern. But I'm not the same.

DANGEROUS CREATURES

Desperate people lined up in an alley.
And where is our allegory of abundance?
Lovely Simonetta squeezing milk from her nipple!
Desperate dreams for simple soup!

Watch that seven-headed dragon!
And here comes the angel with the key to the abyss.
And what of that thing that intoxicates officials!
That monstrous craving for more and more!

Alchemist in search of the philosopher's stone!
I'm with you, Abigail! They *are* dangerous creatures!
They say a glass of water and a piece of bread! Then go to bed.
A hand extended out for a gift!

Devil if they know what to do with it.
They think it may be the great enigma.
No sympathy, no empathy.
The emptiness is as heavy as the fullness.

Ah, a cup of tea! But what's on the plate?
Of late the riddle of the Sphinx! Dirty dishes in the sink!
Very desperate people lined up in an alley.
Just remember I don't rally and I don't believe in fate.

Christopher Martin

MARCESCENCE

I hike a horse trail, tread moss and mire west of Kennesaw Mountain,
cross Noses Creek's crumbling banks. I stop, rest, sit on a rotting log
where stone piles of Confederate earthworks cover the ground,
testaments to what this place has seen, remnants of what it has been.
Here the woods are white, brittle with leaves still clinging to beech trees.
From a fallen beech, a hermit thrush murmurs, flutters farther into brush
when it sees me. Three whitetail does stand vigilant, in an instant vanish
through dusk, tails flared, one with trembling leaves these branches
will bear until spring, will bear as my own limbs hold whispers stirring,
these stories of what it means to die, yet remain bound to a living thing.

Komal Patel Mathew

BLAMING ATLANTA

Our first June, we parked my new white jeep
on the side street facing your dorm.
It was raining, so you cleared the trunk,
laid out two beach towels, a casserole dish
piled with panang and jasmine rice. Everything,
including my hair, smelled like your home.

*

The day I fell asleep on New Year's Eve
and you didn't call, I decided New York
in August. When you came to visit that March,
I tried not to think about how you forgot
a present for my birthday and Christmas,
not even one card. Instead, I praised God
that New York was blameless in winter,

and later, for the shirt in my trunk
wrapped around your neck and face. We shivered waiting
for chicken and rice on some corner stand off 6th Ave.

*

The morning you moved to Atlanta
I bought a black breakfast tray and
taped our pictures from the Spice Market,
Yankees game, Grimaldi's and the pier:
I didn't want you to eat alone.
But when I couldn't wait any longer, I left you
asleep under butter croissants and cold lattes—

Later you wrote *Sorry, I didn't hear you. I didn't hear you
come in.*

*

I can't remember knowing you in hot weather—
now in Atlanta, with your golden green car

and blue boxers. Everything seems new—
From your window, I can see
your neighbors peel clementines in chunks,
their white porch dappled with juice.
From the woman's ease, the man must be reading
something kind; her hair must smell
like his home.

Alan May

BIOGRAPHY OF JIMMY CARTER

*

All love
say the tree frogs at dusk

*

The Creeks that haunt the fallow fields

*

The satellites singing their songs to Kissinger—
little cold war valentines

*

Give the beekeepers drones
and let them dream of fighting

for a holy land or a confederacy

*

Whatever happens

we wake up in a sweat
The sky blue then red

now black all over   ink black

*

The stars:

little pinholes through which The Light
peeks through

*

The foxes in their holes
the thrashers in their nests

*

All love
say the tree frogs at dusk

Mariana McDonald

UPON VIEWING "MEMORY AS MEDICINE"

> *Atlanta-based...Radcliffe Bailey explores American history and memory to encourage healing and transcendence through art.*
> —*High Museum of Art, 2012*

I hear Harriet singing as the turbid blue landscape surrounds me.
Her steady incantation floats above tuned waters, where hopes
and lives were lost. The clanking of chains on railroad ties
echoes to the glittering sky. Quick notes riff past loud silence.

I hear Leadbelly strumming near the black baby grand,
filled with planets spinning in disarray. Train tracks traveled,
yours and mine. Sheets of music slipped in a treasure chest,
like a man's folded handkerchief dotting his suit.

I hear women laughing as they don their masks.
Mama Wata then and now, ancestors and cousins.
Tintype images and medicine chests, across centuries
and oceans. Women fill them up with life.

I hear Martin speaking in the seven-layered light.
His voice today is Cairo, Damascus, Atlanta,
his red Georgia clay footprints filled with the fresh
diaspora of newcomers chanting sí se puede.

I hear Hank's bat crack the speeding ball, take him where
no one's followed. Magic one cleaning up, beating down,
twirling time and space to make new stories. Tall bats
at the ready for all who try to make us mute.

I hear Radcliffe working as I watch a sea of piano keys,
listening for the sound of cells healing, the rumble of repair
in a nation's gut. Lanterns flash as if to ask in ancient code
Where will you walk? What will you say?

Let my pen be an nkisi, a thing that does things, I ask,
as I walk through the Door of Many Returns, where oars
churn in all directions, and I hear the unmistakable sound
of three hundred million voices.

Patrick McGinn

GOOD AFTERNOON TO ME

good afternoon to me. it is april 30 2010. it is a pretty day. i am having a pretty good day. i have been reading literature and it has been a pretty good day.

      readers of literature like ambiguity. if something means something it doesn't mean very much. if something means more than one thing it means more. if you are not certain what something means it means more. people read to understand. they want their life to have meaning. they like ambiguity.

good evening to me. it is may 4 2010. i have felt rotten most of the day. there is no reason you should be interested in this. but a lot of things are reported that you shouldn't be interested in.

good afternoon to me. it is may 5 2010. i have been reading russian literature. i have been reading turgenev. it is fun to read russian literature. there are a lot of descriptions about peasants. so you get to learn a lot about peasants. it helps to put things in perspective. and it is fun to watch from a distance. it is more fun to watch from a distance. and it is more enjoyable to read about poor people from other countries. it is both down-to-earth and exotic. it is not very fun to be poor though. good writers don't make it look very fun. but it is still fun to read. that can't be helped. they are writers. if they didn't make it a little fun nobody would read it. even the writers of the bible knew this. sometimes. but you might not find it as fun as they did. they liked to write about poor people too.

good morning to me. it is may 10 2010. i still do not have a job. i still have not searched for a job. i still am relatively happy. i still worry about it though. i still worry about being happy. a lot of people worry about it though. you can't help worry about it though.

good evening to me. it is december 11 2010. when you are young they teach you to be fair. when you get older, they teach you to be practical. i wish they would have mentioned the practical side when i was younger. it would have been more fair.

good evening to me. it is november 14 2010. my phone has a video recorder. i rarely use it. my ipod has a video recorder. i rarely use it. my typewriter can hardly do anything. i use it all the time.

good evening to me. it is april 16 2011. i looked at the new york times today. on the front page was a story about people behaving badly. there were two or three stories about people behaving badly. it is good to read the paper. it is good to keep up with things.

good evening to me. it is october 29 2014. it is a fine night to be home and alone and writing. it is a fine night to be writing. it is a fine night to be home and alone and doing it. it is a fine night. it is a fine night in october alone and doing what you want to do. it is nice to be doing what you want to do. it is hard to say how nice it is. it is very nice.

    when you've written and spoken and thought and learned and done that. when you've done that. when you've spoken and thought and written and learned. when that has been done. when there has been the thinking and the speaking and the writing and the learning. when there has been that done and you were the doer of it. when there has been speaking and thinking and learning and writing. when that has all been taken care of. when there has been this and that and the other and back again to the this. when you have returned to the this. when you have returned to the this in front of you. when you have returned. you will know it.

    a dying man's last words are. a dying man's last words. a dying man's last. a dying man's last are. a dying man's last words. a dying man's last. his last words are. dying. last.

    to be a linking verb, or not to be a linking verb. to be linking. to be linking verbally. or not. or not to be linking verbally. to be. or not to be. verbally. linking.

Jessica Melilli-Hand

SPACE CAMP MOON-VIEW

Our workbook said the men who flew to the moon
and saw our round, our perfect planet, blue
faith in the vast black space of pupils, knew
the shape of peace and wept. The blood monsoon
in 'Nam poured through America's moon-croon.
My Lai, unknown to us, too far from view.
Listen, the counselors said, the point is you,
the future, point of view. You'll grow up soon.
Remember. When we jumped on the Moon-Jump,
we understood perspective-shift. Below
our giant feet, arriving parents: stumps,
then ants. We didn't weep. We squished them, though
they loomed back up with every earth-bound thump.
They asked us what we learned. We shrugged. Dunno.

Joseph Milford

HOLY PORN TENDRIL

And it rose and it fell, and pulsed like a wave
    Rushing and bubbling with health
One could say that this carcass, blown with vague breath,
    Lived in increasing itself.

    —Charles Baudelaire, "A Carcass"

I just can't walk home without an affliction
    Always Wallace Stevens or some other flaneur
Some Wordsworth, Leopold Bloom, Baudelaire
    Down Maple Street northbound steepled
In wisteria live oak kudzu angel's trumpets
    Which, as college students, we once tried
To distill as hallucinogenics—don't mess

    With the Datura family of flowering weeds—shamans
Have more reticence than the reverent grader
    Or writer of compositions.
Needing a clear head on a four mile trek
Passing South Ridge apartment complex
    A softball field, the TKE house the beer cans
Littering the unkempt lawn, sofa shredded there

    Taking a left on highway 27 where the sidewalk ends
You begin the trail of the downtrodden hoi polloi
    I look down when I walk, a Baptist thing, I think
No honey, not even locusts, but no Lot's salt
    Heartbreak is the logic: speaking of ashes
I pass the Methodist church, the cemetery, and the accursed
    Walking—always through the Black Forest

Or metaphysical tundra, past the roadkill sanguine
    And the eighteen-wheeled susurrus—the chapel doors
Beckon for Saul or Paul—is my apartment miles away Damascus?
    With its poor wood paneling and $300 pet deposit?
I can't just walk for walking's sake, I must
    Tongue my mind for some slake of poetic line.
I wish I were "Chaplinesque," but the flaneur of that poem,

        Hart Crane, walked off of an ocean-liner.
            Under the rail, crossing a concrete bridge, I notice a disembodied
Videotape tendril between my feet—
        This skein begins exactly where the shoulder
Loses gravel and picks up misdemeanors and maintenance
        Convicts. The weeds pounded down, the "shook"

Of the trash puncture stick impaling
        The community service paydirt—that stab
Then the county bushwhacker spreads
        What the parolees miss into the streets, its
        Confetti. I follow the film, the black celluloid snake
Bridging from Hart Crane to musing on film—
        How did this tape extract itself from its VHS armor

To end muddy among detritus curbside?
        Demographic considered, it's no foreign film—
Even in a college town where some know
        Benuel, Cocteau, or Vigo—yet now I show
My cinematic pedestrianism. This could be *Finding Nemo*
        Purchased at *DOLLAR GENERAL* for a preschooler.
It could be *Gone With the Wind*, but I prefer *Memento*.

        I followed the reel off of its spool—a VHS tape
Is approximately 4 miles long—movies
        And intestines—I should have driven home—until
Its filament ended, still attached, a crude umbilical cord
        To the cassette tape case red plastic black letters entitled:
Dirty Debutante Blowjob Sluts (Roman Numeral) *4*.
        Imponderable the porno tape. Dadaists want bicycle

Wheels on barstools. Art that cannot be hung on walls,
        Urinal manifestos, Duchamps. I found my ars poetic
Days later,
        Driving down highway 27, cars in my path peeled
Asunder—a dervish was disrupting the yellow
        Lines—as drivers parked in the passing lines
I saw it—a tornado of metallic tape adagio

        Above mirage of hot asphalt—dancing boricua—
Could it be the porn? Writhing about in the wind
        With its orifices inside of it? The only porn of God
Now through the elements transcendent? As light cascaded through the film,
        Its black luster like licorice, like tasting sex,

Flailing in traffic, bodies in the celluloid
        A copulation of dust and gust, an alchemy, sleaze

Made celestial in march breeze littered
        With pollen and dogwood petals
The carnal acts in a cascade of afternoon cataracts
        The odalisque tryst guttural dance
Sun-sodomized, wind-ravished
        I knew this was fleshed light—the corporal striate
As all cars pull over and dodge

        The only holy porno tape.

Michael Miller

SINGER ON RIVER STREET, SAVANNAH, GEORGIA

With a few words, did you place her in the front row?
Her eyes, raw from elsewhere, beg your attention.
Perched apart from the rest, she is the hungriest one.

Did she come to see you? Your mind traces back
the last week's sequence – first your text to the drummer
that he passed to the agent, the agent to the booking man,

the booking man's tip that set the newspaper rolling.
The front page displayed you. Whooping, you drank till dawn.
On the quiet nights, awake in your dorm room,

you stare at the sky and dream its machinery.
How many gears does it hold? Can your words conduct them?
Through so many reactions, you took the stage

in this city kept by chance, the blocks that Sherman spared
the backdrop as you tuned and set the tip jar down.
In this room may be connections, the unexpected prize

that the right song or smile brings. The woman watches you
watch her. She swallows, cups her hands for warmth.
You say she sought you, not shelter, that her wet feet wound

past the tall ship, the carriages, the rain-spangled river;
the current you started with your fingers on the pad
has changed the motion of the street here, placed a body

where no body was before. Where does the current
go from here? Does she stay? Depart by dawn?
Everything off stage suspended, you cue the next song.

Judson Mitcham

WEIGHT

My grandson, possible iconoclast
and almost three, means to understand weight,
testing things to see what he can lift,
what he can move. He shoves a box of books.
He hoists a bag of groceries. If he could,
he'd push the sofa across the room. So here we are,
the whole family, in the last days of June,
visiting the Georgia State Capitol–the building
cool and mostly empty; in the rotunda
and elsewhere, marble busts of famous men
on pedestals as heavy as small trucks.
My grandson passes through security and runs
toward where I'm standing,
next to Alexander H. Stephens–immutably white,
his eyes open and blank, the Vice President
of the Confederate States, known for making clear
the cornerstone of his new nation:
the supremacy of the white race. And in his first
oblivious political act, our little Caucasian
throws his shoulder into the stone,
as though to take down that pillar where it stands,
and I pretend to give him a hand, but
I've had my chance.

QUESTION

But if a man falls in the forest,
if he trips over his own feet
and falls out of control,
and if no one else is there
when he thuds to the dirt,
is that man still ridiculous?
And if a train rattles off
into the cool night, miles
from the house, if it quiets
the baby, has it become
a kind of lullaby? If a tree
falls in the forest
         and there is no God
to witness it, and no human
either, is there a question—
when the deer lifts its head
to listen, when the crow
opens the air
with its old raw note, when
the ants and the beetles come
to interrogate the dead one
suddenly upon them?

Maren O. Mitchell

LEARNING HOW TO KILL

Piss, crazy, ghost, sugar: evolved from wasps,
the only other creature to herd for food,

they crouch like mammals to drink,
bathe with the grace of cats.

Extreme Communists, they change sex, sprout wings
for the good of the whole.

Sick nest survivors emigrate, forsaking family.
Hearing the warmth of spring they invade early,

flowing back and forth along my windowsill,
up and down mini-vases of pansies and thyme,

laying chemical trails: *Aphids ahead! Good milking!*
Casual across a hot stove,

they stagger out of microwave minutes with nothing
but slight brain damage.

Kept fresh in the fridge for days, they move faster than I do.
The freezer stops them dead in their tracks.

They fall for the false sweetness of Pepsodent,
become muscle-bound unscrewing the cap,

dizzy from navigating threads.
They reconnoiter a cache of "stevia," sugar x 300,

sweeter than all the perfumes of Arabia.
With sheepish smiles whitened by traces of the forbidden,

they offer cocaine to their Queen,
foreseeing her fashionable waistline,

her rise among her peers.
Across counters, with 70% alcohol, I swipe

devastation through orderly fat-foraging ranks.
They retreat in routs from the big "it."

Marching lines spin drain-ward,
fighting up against the down.

Not a picnic, I kill from all angles.
I see no faces, slaughter with ease.

Finding one alone I roll it to
death between thumb and forefinger.

Within days my soul has sprung a leak,
compassion escaping at an alarming rate.

Fearing afterlife, I grant intermittent mercy,
rescue with oar finger those drowning,

blow others into legendary flights to be recounted by their descendants.
Research tells me more than I want to know.

Fooled by compulsive bathing,
the salmonella, the pseudomonas they carry are news.

Prudent, they import golden Mr. Clean-smelling resin,
sterilize feet before crossing their thresholds.

Instinct kicks in; rescues cease.
Guilt recedes. I know murder.

Sally Stewart Mohney

AND WHAT OF CAMELLIAS

now it is spring
and off-season
for blossom?

Whom will you call
and talk to at great
length, about how
Atlantans butcher
crepe myrtles?

*They need to grow up
then hang down,*
your mother
long advised,
like an umbrella.

Decreed by Grandma, too,
who grew up in a teeny town
in north Georgia.

This has long since been
a family generational thing:

*There can be nothing sudden,
 about a camellia in bloom,
 nor pruning a crepe.*

Sheer poetry
and patience,
abound.

From what you can recall
they had some negativity
toward crepes, sasanquas,
and all things South Carolina.

Peaches too puny to bother with,
Grandma Vesta exhaled.

Who is there now to dredge up
and ask about the particular
peculiar climate, and as to what thrives?

Yesterday at the wholesale nursery
you bought a puny, pink peony.

For she who passed,
last May.

Janice Townley Moore

EVENING OUT
Atlanta, 1952

On days too hot for breath to be easy
my father left his desk in the cellar
to drive our Easter ducks, full grown,
to Piedmont Park for a swim.
Crated up in the trunk of our pea-green Plymouth,
they quaked and quacked the long three miles.
Our whole family went along for the show.
Without coat and tie my father sprawled
in the cool by the lake. I remember
how his wallet bulged in his back pocket
as he bent to unlatch the crate.
No pounding joggers then, only walkers slow as July
and a few children ringing the bells on their bikes.
A quiet crowd inched forward to see the ducks
gliding over the dark reflections of magnolias,
sometimes flapping their wings
with the sound of sheets in the wind.
After paddling among the fallen petals,
they shored up for recrating,
lured by lettuce, as I watched
the late sun glinting off my father's black shoes
sinking into the red clay bank.

Tony Morris

A MILLION FANS

--And there you stood in your gold lamé,
hushed voice a whispered rub of fine sand.

All shimmy and shake that boy could rattle and jive,
    some trashy, east Tupulo public housing kid playing
  hillbilly Acuff, Rogers, Snow who'd swallowed
        enough Sister Rosetta Tharpes' liquid, rolling,
gospel "Down by the Riverside," and rode the line
    of Rufus Thomas's "Memphis Train far enough
to answer Eddie Bonds' *you're never*
        gonna make it as a singer, with that's alright,
I'm gonna put on my blue suede shoes and hang
    out at the heartbreak hotel until I pick
  up the handles *Hillbilly Cat, Memphis Flash, King*
        of Western Bop, and when I forget to remember
to forget, I'll put Rock-n-Roll atop the Billboard charts
    make guitar the lead and sing like a jug
  of corn liquor at a champagne party in Vegas
        while the critics treat me like a hound dog
and the fans love me tender, jamming
    with Jerry Lee Lewis and Carl Perkins layin'
down a rattle and roll leg pivot that'll get 'em all shook
        up—too much, they said, don't baby, don't,
till the army and prescribed amphetamines
    pushed that finger-picking, double-stop slide
  acoustic boogie, blues-based bent-note,
        single-string work out of the back rooms
and onto the big stage—then momma died
    and you knew it was now or never to marry
  that hard-headed Priscilla or you'd be lonesome
        tonight and every night, so ten top ten's later
and lost in Hollywood, all suspicious minds
    and Kentucky rain for a man whose raw,
  slurred two and a half octave range
        of tender whispers to sighs that ran up to shouts,
grunts, grumbles and gruffness and could move
    you from surrender to fear, "like busting out of jail"
  said Dylan, that burning love, that wailing,

                ecstatic, reckless sound pushed out in orgasmic
gyrations opening the door of black culture
        to the mainstream, said Little Richard, integrator,
    blessing, changed everything, said Bernstein
            a revolution the sixties came from, and he fell
from, until the talentless impersonators, the black
       velvet paintings were only perverse traces
   of the great rocker, heart throb, teddy bear,
              purveyor of schlock who could still make us itch
like a man on a fuzzy tree, wild as a bug, and in love.

Eric Nelson

GEORGIA SUNSET

How scarred we are, how familiar
With hospitals and humiliation
And the gloved hands of strangers.
Love is everything and everything
Is not enough. The telephone rings
To death and all we can do is answer.

Flying back from your mother's
Funeral in the city where every road
Once led to us, above the knuckled
Mountains where we lived long enough
To always long for them,

Down the coast to the sea level hot-house
That is the only home our children know,
I watch the plane's shadow
Tracking us, hugging the landscape
Across valleys, ridges, clay, swamp.

Landing, I recall taking off
Into a gorgeous setting sun
That never set as we flew towards it,
Westward, time moving backward.

Jeff Newberry

PRAYER AFTER A RARE SOUTH GEORGIA SNOW

Call the cold *apocalyptic*. *Useasonable*.
                     A vortex of arctic chance.

Call it *climate change* or *End of Days*.
                     Call them *unfortunate*, those packed

in a stalled school bus on I-75.
                     The children who once prayed

for a snow day watch the world bleach.
                     Call black ice *natural*,

the lines of cars & trucks *inevitable*.
                     Call us *unprepared*.

Call frozen top soil a *tragedy*.
                     Call our pleas *platitudes*.

But hear, oh hear our words
                     feathering from frosted lips,

voices rising to a sky   silent as snow.

Laurah Norton

MIDSHIPMEN

We know this all summer. We know it
all year. Atlanta: landlocked.
No sibilant slide off into
the sea. Rest evades.
Moisture settles into our
pores, our joists, our creaking starboard.

We smell of gasoline, of hot pavement,
of salty unease. Atlanta has burned
us down, out, into our essential aspect—
all our dreams, expatriate. Our
expectations have cut teeth.

We own this place and its disappointments.
Our prospects have sunk into
the loamy earth. Seasick, we cling onto
the edges of the map. We were promised
a way out. Our smiles crack
the corners.

Our son, five months: a photograph.
He is surrounded by gravel;
the straggling grass offers an apologetic
frame. Though clay is little
birthright, he is native to this
place. Positioned in his
father's lap, he is surrounded.

Marooned, we might have chosen
dignity, but instead we offer this:
our fair Atlantan, in August white—
inheritor of detritus, of tar, of depreciated
values. He does not know enough
to fear this place, and yet, he clings—
all instinct. We link arms to show we are
not adrift. Serious, he squints into the surging
heat, and, perhaps, into that distant sea.

Nick Norwood

CLAMOR

The mill's non-stop noise, a whir and a clangor,
follows him home, over the bridge and up
the hill, while at his back it goes on wheezing,
chuffing lint through manifold windows,

into the village with the lunch bucket knocking
at his knee, to bounce a kid on his knee
in the sunlit parlor of the four-room cottage
identical to the one next door, next door

to the river that powers the turbines. The privy's
sulfurous stench stretches to the porch while
his own open windows pass heat and flies
and rugrats flap through the sprung screen door.

A rung up from the tenant shack, maybe two
from a hovel on the Rhine, a hut on the Liffey,
the Mersey, the Volga, he is equal now
to the terrace-house bloke in Wigan,

to his next-century brother in Coimbatore,
or the one in a cinder-block flat in Nantong
perched above the Yangtze, whose mill tunes
its waters daily to the color it's dyeing—

red, blue, purple—through a little trap door.

THE TIE-SNAKE
Chattahoochee River, Columbus, Georgia

Muscogee knew a serpent hid
below the falls in deep water,
glimpsed the Tie-Snake's shadow
beneath the churn and tread.

Spade head solemn as a sphinx.
Untold lengths of scale and strength
coiled and ready to wrap limbs
of fishers and diggers of clams.

Lover who loves only one thing:
to lie with others forever under
froth, amid the crag and gleam
of boulders, the mist-rise and vapor.

Still a handful every year.
A glut of screams, the river's roar
rafters and kayakers paddle over,
ecstatic in their plastic gear.

Christina Olson

LAST LOVE LETTER FOR AUTUMN

In 2007, a Vanity Fair *editor spent months tracking down the location of the Windows desktop image* Autumn.

A quiet lane. A sentry of sugar
maples wearing hunter orange.

The perfect, weathered barn.
Had he asked me, I could

have told him: it's nice two
weeks a year. Then comes

the raking. Palms red, weeping
blisters. Once, I thought

I loved a man in Vermont.
We had white sweaters.

We drove Route 9 and ate
butterbrickle. At the north lake

where the monster lives,
that pretty college town,

we almost convinced ourselves
our lives would matter.

And now I'll never have
to say *leaf-peeper* again,

or pretend to like the grit
of buckwheat. No more

lunches of slick orange soup.
Down here, ladies dress up

for football. The men don
belts embossed with dogs

and eagles and tigers. Pumpkins
slump in eighty degree heat.

Trick or treating on a beach.
You can get used to anything.

On the way back from the coast,
I see the fields have erupted

in cotton. When I squint,
it almost looks like snow.

Lee Passarella

IMMANENCE

Antibellum Plantation, Stone Mountain Park, Georgia

We leave the one-room schoolhouse
with the double meaning of its woodenness
spelled out in ranks of hair-shirt oaken
benches and plank-top desks without a blemish
of utility. No inkwells, no pencil minders to give
them purpose. It is a place of the truly elementary—
of bone-tired inertia and of rote, and educative homilies
about the patriot saints. On the slatted wall
above the teacher's desk, the Father of His Country
still presides from the unfinished portrait
by Gilbert Stuart. Disembodied head, dead white
on a black ground of rusty satin. It speaks to dark eternity,
bright virtue: the mythic cherry tree; the bitter winter
of faithfulness, Philadelphia locked up like an English gaol;
the patience to stick till the screw turned tight
at Yorktown. Did the hardness *or* the homilies prepare
those boys of 1850 for Sunday strolls to come,
ranked like Continentals, into the rifle's obliterating jaws?

My wife has four-leaf clover on her mind.
I've never seen one, and she abhors the vacuum
of my skepticism. She prays that God will let us find
this unicorn of flora, and as we walk the well-groomed lawn,
she plucks one up, a tiny Intercession. Yet there's another:
I stoop, incredulous, and here it is, the four plump lobes
like the fingers of a cartoon hand. I laugh the sinner's
incongruous guffaw, while she thanks God, He
who helps our unbelief. I think how I want to be with *her*
when lightning X-rays open spaces, or the car knifes
across four lanes of highway, the shattering median,
the onrushing flail of steel. Then I recall those war-
dead Southern boys, bent to their hard-assed catechism,
their Calvinist Lives of the Saints—
three hundred thousand war-dead boys.

For now, I take my little cache of Immanence
and press it in a book, a fragile homily
between the pages of a novel, *nouvel,* new.

Lynn Pedersen

WHY WE SPEAK ENGLISH

Because when you say *cup* and *spoon*
your mouth moves the same way as your grandfather's
and his grandfather's before him.
It's Newton's first law: A person in motion
tends to stay in motion with the same speed
and direction unless acted upon by an unbalanced force—
scarcity or greed.
Is there a word for greed in every language?

Because the ear first heard
dyes furs pepper ginger tobacco cotton timber
silk freedom horizon
and the tongue wanted to taste
all these fine things.

And when my son asks why his father speaks Danish
and he and I speak English and Carlos—
at kindergarten—speaks Portuguese:

because Denmark is and has always been.
Our ancestors tracked north and Carlos'
tracked south. What's left in their wake
is language.

Because it comes down
to want, to latitude and longitude as ways to measure
desire, invisible mover of ships—
great clockwise gyre of water in the sea—
like some amusement park ride where boats seem to sail
but run on tracks under the water.

Because to change course now would be like diverting
the Arno, this centuries-long rut we've dug ourselves
into, and how would it be to wake up one morning
with bird *oiseau* or another word entirely?

Oliver T. Perrin

TOMORROW

How your face
has changed.

It seems only yesterday
you were the guardian
of childhood, whispering
"nevermind" and "one day".

Little girls with candy
in their fat sticky fists…

Were you to uncloak yourself
the nursery rhymes would stop.

My mother would pause
with that air of having
heard the household ghost,
while dead birds
fall from the sky,
thudding against the roof
like hailstones.

Patrick Phillips

BLUERIDGE BESTIARY

1. Vulture

Business never slows for the air's ubiquitous
morticians, their spiraling so effortless

we might admit its beauty, if we didn't know
how eagerly, in those ridiculous black boas,

they wait to begin the endless dissipation
we take as proof: we've been forsaken,

unable to believe our angels of deliverance
rise even to the murky heaven of catfish.

2. Catfish

Greedy face of the zoot-suited villain
in a movie, sharpening his dagger-thin

moustache: sonsabitches I'd wish against
each time the bobber ducked and danced—

who swallowed all my best lures whole
and hissed, as with the crusted needle-nose

I ripped the hook and the hooked heart out
of a thousand, gasping cotton mouths.

3. Cottonmouth

The cure for life, said Socrates, is dying.
The cure for snakebite: slice your skin,

suck poison then, the guidebook says, breathe
easily as the viper glides through brittle leaves.

A pit in its face can see your thudding heart.
Its flicked tongue tastes you sweating in the dark.

And even the severed head strikes with venom,
as if death's never dead, just playing possum.

4. Possum

Of all the corpses, none's more easily forgotten
than those bellies strewn along the roadside. Rotten

entrails flaking into the treads of tires,
dark shapes hunkered on the low-slung wires

as the whole scene flares in that quick brightness
through which we hurtle past the oracle, oblivious

of what it means to see them suffer
and rise from ashes on the wings of vultures.

Stephen Roger Powers

THE MONA LISA IN SPAIN KNOWS WHY I CAN'T COME IN THE SIDE DOOR ANYMORE

Underneath a copy of a masterpiece,
sketches and first tries might wait
five hundred years for a curious
art historian at the Prado to expose
them with infrared reflectography
and unearth them from below the picture
we've come to know. Dolly Parton
will make us wait forever to see
what she's revised under her
make-up, years and years of fly
paper layered on an animation cell.
At this point she might as well try erasing tattoos
if she doesn't want to be Dolly Parton anymore.
Notice it's only copies we examine
so probingly, not originals. Keep in mind a tattoo
comes from below. So does a scar. A needle and a knife
are simply conjurers, not creators, of the first
sketches trapped under the picture,
which means that someday somebody dissecting
my mummified heart will find your fingerprints
still on the lock of the side door, and the burned out
tealights left on my stomach when I fell asleep.

Randy Prunty

VINCA MINOR

dream: i was a ground cover, maybe *vinca minor*, and i had rhizomatic toes.

interpretation: wanting and having instead of thinking and making.

consequence: any edge is a precipice.

consequence: allergies now but purple accents come summer.

interpretation: as ground cover doesn't really stand, so much as creep, and since a good Lacanian must speak of the knot that is *minor*, then one must begin to worry, if not openly rue.

background: i think i may have seen the journal Rhizome on my bookshelf yesterday.

background: *vinca minor* is one of those plants you have to decide whether it's a helpful friend or an invasive stranger.

consequence: ground and abound go post-rhyme.

interpretation: lack of a proper object.

background: i hate purple.

interpretation: if the big toe had evolved as opposable instead of the thumb we'd be walking on our hands.

consequence: none.

consequence: looking out this window i can't see past the pane of glass. i know the glass is clear and beyond the window is a dust-cracked garden, a see-saw, and a street (i can hear cars) but i can't see those things. all i can see is the clear clear glass.

consequence: i cannot not write periwinkle.

interpretation: it's not surprising i had trouble in elementary school with its rows of empty faces and shadowless lights and wire mesh in the windows and the only color was the faded cut-outs of red apples in green ivy around the ashy-white blackboard.

consequence: i dig it up roots and all to make a statement.

Wyatt Prunty

TWO VIEWS

    1
Into the laterals and faults of strata
Whose linear seams are like memory,
Water wades its way, settling matters
In small aquifers, incised meanders;
Then floods over a landscape that teaches
Plains are only so much sediment,
Silt the slow ocean of any reach.

Think travertine and serpentine mantel-
high in living rooms, or kames and tills
Scattered like loose change, the marvelous marble
Of dolomite and metamorphic rock,
Or granite now as coolingly aloof
As someday overhead . . . small seismic self
Feeling a gust rattle years through the roof.

Meanwhile, there's still the phone and mail, the door,
And the reassuring fact the fault's not yours
As you've not budged. Not even the cat crosses the floor.
Outside, the world's continuum of nests
Is full of cries announcing differences,
While mineshaft down, the brittle shale of self
Waits, certain of its own circumferences.

One is colossus of one's growing doubt,
With ideas like past presidents profiled
And floating enthusiastic shouts
From old elections, conclusions of the will,
The dehydrations of mere permanence.
But high wing over shadow, how the world
Doubles in its transience.

    2
Resplendently fragile, more color than weight,
As agile of flight as of changed habitat,
The birds are choric in the fate
Of their varieties; predictable

Of habit and Darwinian choices,
Myriad on one scale, and on another
Essential and of but one in all. And voices,

This side liquid whistles followed by a trill,
While there, a series of clear carolings,
Then the rapid whinnies of descending will
While somewhere overhead a finch attempts
All notes at once, as though to summarize
The way limbs ladder up, step green to blue
So shadows rise.

But year on year, wing beat and season,
Fattened or starved, silent or full
Of migratory sass, one reason
Brings each back, whether the same or no—
Warbler and thrush, sparrow and finch, wren, jay,
Thrasher and dove, tanager, waxwing, owl, crow, hawk . . .
They light, feed, breed, migrate or stay.

Calendar wise in their brief histories
And vulnerable as any emigrants
Searching to eat, they are geographies
Of days, convergences of now,
And needed if for nothing more than their arrival
When, worthy that again we crane to see,
They bring survival.

Janisse Ray

ELEVENTH

I know where
the ribbon snake
lives—
under the maple
by the barn.
One day when I
was there
a dead leaf
crackled like fire
and I saw her,
slip of green
I followed
around the waist
of the tree,
through already
dying grass.
When she turned
to face me, eyes
burning, she
studied me.
I – wanting
to feel her softness,
her certainty, the stove
of her tiny heart –
touched one finger,
only one,
upon her perfect tail.
At that moment
the tree opened
and she wound
inside, her
passageway
dark and narrow.
Long before
she turned away,
no doubt,
she lay
on her mat of earth

at the bottom
of the maple,
among the roots,
strip
of brilliant
kindling.
The eleventh
commandment is
love the earth,
love the tree,
love the snake.

Andrea Rogers

THE DUPE

> *The fact is, people don't know their own faces. Half of 'em have never looked in a glass half a dozen times in their life, and directly they see a pair of eyes and a nose, they fancy they are their own.*
> —Street portrait photographer to Henry Mayhew in
> London's East End, 1850s

A slight-framed woman prepares
her face from memory – a glass,

for her, a rare and shining bird.
Arranging her hat by feel,

she comprehends herself in segments:
the slice of an eye in the pitcher,

a body perched on the river's lip.
She must assemble what she can

from memory, glance toward
the callers, agree or disagree.

In the studio, she pays
for her sitting, poses

unnaturally in the light,
face flat as a shallow well.

If she flinches, she could blur
the features beyond recognition,

a ghostlike trail of women's faces,
the self fleeing the long exposure.

If she flinches, the photographer
will find a similar "specimen"

in the display window, with a dress
like hers, in half-mourning. He will

send her home clutching someone
else's proof, which she will take at face

value, a face that will never be
any closer to her own.

Rosemary Royston

WHERE I'M FROM
after George Ella Lyon

Always a state line nearby, a lake, pine trees.
Border towns with only one or two traffic lights
full of people who know each other

from grade school through their senior year,
who live with two generations on plots of land
with cows, chickens, or turkeys, where kids drive

four-wheelers or stick-shifts by the age of 10,
towns with names like Elberton, Lincolnton,
and Inman, where my family and I were given

a brick ranch-style parsonage with pea-green
living room sets, a slab of concrete for a patio,
a garden spot. I'd know the people of those small

places for five years, at most. Sunday service
at Coldwater, Cokesbury, or New Bethel Methodist.
Covered-dish dinners outside, granite headstones

nearby. Every pew had brown hymnals, pencil stubs
for pledge cards. I'd sing the *Doxology*, kneel
for communion. Surrounded by people, I pretended

to join in prayer. What I loved was the softness
of soil when my bare feet sank into the freshly tilled
garden and, as I grew braver, the woods,

climbing trees and disappearing into webs and clouds.

James Sanders

EMORY EPIPHYTE #2

Mike Saye

STORM PIT

Ignore the dirt daubers' crumbling cigars
and the fallen beams just through the door.

See where my grandmother's grandpa
gathered all the boys on this side of the hill

and shoveled a twelve-foot room, eight feet deep
in a bank, laid creosote cross-ties for the roof

and stacked marble from scrap pilfered
at the Tate quarry to frame the door.

Everyone kept an oil lantern by the bed,
and when the squall line slapped the pines down,

easy as a switch across a boy's legs, the family
bolted through sheets of rain to get to the pit.

They listened for the jenny's bray, waited
to hear her stop, struck dead—animals draw

lightning—knowing they'll burn the carcass
where it lands, and run the risk of witches,

drawn to light their pipes off burning horses.

Emily Schulten

STONE FRUIT

You used to bring fruit to bed
after we'd make love,
stone fruit – a plum or a peach.
Naked, we took turns
biting away the skin,
until the pit exposed itself.

Apple was once a generic term
to describe different fruits,
even some vegetables and nuts.
Tomatoes were called love-apples.

You succumbed to temptation,
skewed what it meant to be yours.

In my *Children's Bible*
Adam and Eve beneath tree-canopies
look toward and away from each other.
It wasn't hard, I don't think,
for them to share that apple
(or was it even an apple at all?)
when all they knew
was each other, gardens,
and snakes. When we tasted
the nectar that clung to the stone-center
there was nothing sweeter than
the last tastes of not knowing.

Ron Self

ROMEO AND JULIET OF THE CHATTAHOOCHEE

Ancient Romeo and his plump Juliet
walk along the river bank holding hands
in the pale sunlight of this November day
"where we lay our scene." No Capulet or Montague,
"both alike in dignity," shall keep them apart.
Mercutio and Tybalt are dead. Friar Lawrence
has yet to stick his long nose
into love's sweet amorous business.

So they stroll together, both "past our dancing days,"
stop occasionally, turn toward one another,
look with longing into eager star-crossed eyes
blind to Romeo's thin gray hair, his arthritic knees,
Juliet's plainness, her avoirdupois,
see only love going toward love,
teaching "torches to burn bright."
"Stony limits cannot hold love out."

Romeo tells Juliet she is beautiful,
"snowy dove trooping with crows,"
"beauty too rich for use, for earth too dear."
Juliet tells Romeo he is her knight in shining armor.
"Speak again, bright angel," he whispers.
Sparrows and pewits twitter in the trees.
"At lover's perjuries, they say Jove laughs."
"You kiss by the book," Juliet says to Romeo
as he succumbs to that "trespass sweetly urged,"
takes her in his arms, as much of her
as his arms are capable of encircling.

Against backdrop of river cascading over rocks,
Juliet poses for a picture, fills the camera lens
from side to side for she is "wide as a church door."
Romeo, wanting a close up, comes closer,
but also wanting all of her in the picture,
steps back, and back and still farther back
to snap the shot. "One more to be safe," he says,
and Juliet leans out over the river's edge,
lifts all her chins, smiles sweetly,

recalling for Romeo the "prodigious birth of love,"
that made him forswear his name, transported him
"past hope, past cure, past help"
made him "fortune's fool," "worm's meat."

But "what's in a name," he thought.
"A rose by any other name would smell as sweet,"
and then he noticed that fair Juliet was gone,
her "so light a foot" had disappeared
from camera lens, from river bank, and was
even then sailing "upon the bosom of the air,"

soon to sink beneath the waves
where ancient Romeo's "world-wearied flesh"
considered not going at all, but, he jumped in
to save her anyway, sealing with his final breath
"a dateless bargain to engrossing death."

Oh, do not laugh at "adversity's sweet milk, philosophy."
"He jests at scars who never felt a wound."
"But, soft! What light though yonder window breaks?"
"Jocund day stands tiptoe on the misty mountaintops."
"Parting is such sweet sorrow." "Come, let's away."

Nancy Simpson

MY FATHER TOLD ME

He was at a Snapfinger Creek picnic,
eating his first peanut butter
when he first saw an airplane in the sky.
Age fifteen, absorbed
in the theory of light, I asked him,
"Is light electrons or waves?" If this
confused scientists for centuries,
why did Coach French want me to learn
the debate in six weeks. I couldn't see it
As father told his story, I heard the engine
of the first plane to fly above Atlanta,
high, behind a far cloud,
At that time in my life, I wanted to probe
how the mind can travel fast as
the speed of flight, and how happy the body
when the mind is somewhere else.
There are no photos from Snapfinger Creek,
but there is one shot of my young father,
radiant in the red glow of sunset.
This is no picnic. Show me the x-ray.
I can see it now. Light streams
as energy waves, flowing, healing the body.
I get it, but of course, I am older.

James Malone Smith

SMARTMOUTH AT LARGE

Teachers testified to my chronic tartiness,
although I swore myself incapable of such a think.

No warning of his presents, my father
froze me often in some mouthing-off additude.

Even the demure piano lady
insisted I damper those squawky sharps.

"Take lunch," one boss always said. So I did.

Many plangent persons spoke to undo misery
(and thus my decision to grow older on my own),

everybody convinced I would loose
hard earned money, do nothing worthwild,

even though they made sure I was well bread.

It's like a Brueghel, isn't it?
Everyone in on the act.

SMARTMOUTH AND THE MYSTERIES

Year upon year I know less and less
about time. It gits like nobody's business,

though I suspicion it is not. Verily,

I am content with dust snug in corners.
I wander around scroungy as John the Baptist.

And no longer implored to worship anything,
free of idol chitchat, I snoop about the premises.

At Easter Vigil the priest has angels at the tomb
and a *mirthquake*. Shaken, he addressed

the State of the Jungian, and God's rabbity
elbow in my ribs made me jump and yelp.

So when I read in a caption, "Maryland woman
now Buddhist lama," I hear my often-

misquoted mother driving her enormous car.

R. T. Smith

ALPHABET

In the sewing room
the mail-order Singer
with its chrome-rimmed
wheel and gleaming needle
was turned under
to make a desk while
mother started dinner.

I faced west where
the window shimmered.
For an hour I rehearsed
my letters, spelling
everything visible –
zipper and scissors,
thimbles and spools.
The oval mirror made
the wallpaper zinnias
flower still further,
and a mantel clock
held the minutes back.

The Eagle pencil,
smelling of cedar
in my cramped hand,
scratched fishhook
j or an *l* like a needle.
Late sunlight glazed
the holly leaves silver
beyond the peeling sill.
While I squinted hard
at the Blue Horse paper,
the twilight world
held perfectly still.

When I was finished,
each curve and flourish
set in disciplined rows,
fresh tea with ice

appeared at my elbow,
the yellow *C* of lemon
in the tumbler's perfect *O*,
and if mother had praise
for what I had done,
I would shine all evening
bright as a straight pin,
while the new moon
with its careless serifs
cleared the trees, and rose.

READING GROUPS

Five Blackbirds sulked in the corner circle,
Slow with books, Miss Noonan claimed.
Cardinals and Robins around the room
crooned and cackled at the antics
of Dick and Puff and prissy Jane
for extra milk and tinfoil stars
while my flock struggled. We read
aloud or doodled. I preferred
Genesis, Grit, The Atlanta Constitution
("Covers Dixie Like the Dew"),
reports of train wrecks,
Lester Maddox, Tech football
and barbecues. *Stop that cloud
gathering*, her stern voice said.
Her plastic ruler slapped my hand,
but I was elsewhere, wind-borne, flying.
The welt across my palm burned red
as the rose on a blackbird's wing.

Gregory Vincent St. Thomasino

MERCURY

passing
and that it may, falls, go on

the one to revolve upon the other.
Passing, go on

falls
and here reverses.

Are so to pass or call or day, are lines
no longer to be called

are so to speak, and write
or so to draw a woman

a voice, a personality, a style of dresses
of new acquaintances and of places.

Passing
falls outside, are difficult to call

to land the one upon the other
passing, go on

falls
and that it may, in all reverses

ANSELM

seeming, as it does, in doing so, to
or,

are capable, and possessing
of invention

stringing fables, and pickets
diversion, and demonstration

a tailor, or teacher
often, taking person

or,
various purposes and means

and men and beginnings
various beginnings

A pose, or situation
in view, both of houses, and cars

cities, and scaffolding
the welcome, and valediction

and earn us, at last
of motive, or character, are certain

ordinary and visible attractions
are certain visible attractions

being named, and neighboring
himself, and someone else

can smile, easily and well
and curious, and silent

John Stephens

SCENT OF ASH

I lay in the patch of dirt where I picked the last cherry
tomatoes, autumn passed its rustle through the trees,
delivering its winded unrest. Morning air
like iced tea, yellow-orange leaves fall
like sheets of tissue paper. A row of sunflowers
flash their vision.

I dream with the car windows down, Dylan plays
on the radio, tells me, *A hard rain is gonna fall.*
A sign reads, YIELD. Someone comes flying by,
a scarecrow runs through the patch,
disappears, like last summer's heat.

In a dirt lot, stacks of split oak sit next
to the price for BOILED PEANUTS. Here she stokes
the fireplace, which once warmed a day glow room.
She is streams of smoke that take their gritty march,
ash wisps ignite the air. It's her hearthly
breath that beckons me.

Todd Stiles

GHOST TRAIN

That night I was thinking about the flashpoint
of gummy bears, or maybe it was ectoplasm
breaking through, a sticky reminder
that there wouldn't be enough room
on the trestle for soul and body
to squeak through this one still entwined.

Had I known that gambling my retirement on
ecto derivatives, the pursuit of that intangible
iron horse, would result in a 3 a.m. collision
of desire and fatal kinetic force, I might have
opted for a simpler passion: Comic collecting.
Writing poetry. Cross stitch.

But no, I bit off my hunk of glory and chewed for all
I was worth, wearing my lactose invulnerability into
that final encounter. Even as fate bore down on me
and my unseen legs pumped in the dark, I regretted none of it.

The keys to Pancake City are mine now, and the ticker-tape
parade goes on and on. That's me in front leaning off
the engine, beaming as all the trains that ever haunted
stretch to the horizon, welcoming me with one long wail.

Leon Stokesbury

NEMEROV'S "A PRIMER OF THE DAILY ROUND" HELD AS A MIRROR UP TO NATURE

A peels an apple, while B kneels to God...

What, for instance, do you suppose might prove to be
the significance if I were to dismiss class fifteen minutes
early tonight, and each of you, as you stride out
into the descending purple cloaks of dim and gloom,
each of you reaching your separate parking lots
just a bit lighter, because of this slight but sudden
surprising slip of time, each of you igniting
your Probes, Infinitis, Mirages and Charades,
and tooling back into traffic beneath the Cimmerian dusk—
what, now, might the import prove to be,
as you stream toward your various destinations
surrounded by a completely different array of vehicles
than if I had set you free at the usual 7:30
rather than at 7:15?
                        And what consequence might
you claim if the car in the lane next to you, odd car,
bad car, old Chevy Malibu, swerves into your lane
creating a decidedly unpleasant union and—
in the same way a concrete bust of Elvis placed upon
a three-foot concrete pedestal in your own backyard
becomes the emerald ivy that it's set among,
and like the October umbra of oak and pine that
concrete bust of Elvis rests beneath becomes that bust
of Elvis in return—your bumpers intertwine,
commingling beneath the bleak, black sky?

And as you stumble enraged from your, say, cream
blue Avalon, you see with such clarity the immediately
beloved other—trembling, stunned, numb—not at all
the jousting argumentative you had pre-conceived,
and as you stand there, lonely two, at the murky center
of an empty ocean, exchanging State Farm insurance cards,
telephone numbers too, you hold the two cards
in your hand, side by side, thinking these insurance cards
are like these cars, conjunctive, these cars like the two

of us, or they could be, couldn't they, you think,
and cast a quick glimpse as she slides, but slowly, back
inside: Latin eyes and lashes, looking down, skin
shining, silk beneath her rusty Malibu's interior lighting—
things can become analogous, can't they, by being
placed in tandem, just by happening in a line.
                                                   You
want only to forgive her, now, to let her know she
has already been forgiven, and to ask her to forgive
you, not for what you've done, but what you would do
someday, in some distant year, distant town, grit
in the bed, the incessantly noisy motel ice machine
across the hall—and for a second you are sure she
would, if you asked, if only you were not too yaller-
yaller-yaller-bellied to begin. Why, even art holds up
such random linkages, you almost say: *Hail in August,
Landscape with Summer Snow, Desert Rain.*
                                          But
the moment is gone, ephemeral, little powdery flecks
of glaze falling off the doughnut of the world. *Young
Man with Thumb Up Butt.* And now she is smiling,
apologizing again. O my contiguous, you think, O
my juxtaposed!
                 She looks down once more, then drives
away pocked and pounded, but able, it seems, to negotiate
her path amongst the massive, dark turbidity. And thus
it begins. A week goes by. Your nerve returns. Then
you do call; ask her to dinner. And a year goes by
before you marry, and then nine years, ten years total
from this very night, from my releasing you into
the desultory caprice of evening, O my adjacents,
ten years before the blood and public pain and lies
and her living somewhere close to Albuquerque last
you heard. But still you remember those long lashes
looking down: *Still Life with Red Pepper:* handing you
her State Farm insurance card, as if it were this very
night, tonight, which it is, the vision undiminished,
strong, like that lingering zing left on the tongue
from a more-than-acceptable Gorgonzola—
and then it is you recall this lecture, remember
these fifteen minutes, discerning what consequence
might be claimed: nightshade, scimitar, guillotine,
what future plans for gunfire brought to bear.

                                                            So,
go now, my tangentials, wind your weary ways
out amidst this mere shank of the gloaming,
children in an autumn garden, orphans in a storm,
with night dew dripping off the wilting topiary—
some toward domiciles, some to perform your brazen
stand-ups and sit-downs in the gin joints of your choosing—
little molten ingots marching as to war, two by two,
considering, perhaps, the essential nature of side meat
to the American breakfast. Green eggs and ham.
The comic genius of Curly Howard. *Nude at the Window.*
Study in Burnt Sienna. The Menaced Assassin.
The Persistence of Memory. Twilight's Last Gleam.

INTO THE FURTHEST REGIONS

> *The enough is the largest land animal.*
> —freshman essay

We managed to hire some indigenous
to carry our assorteds, and so trekked forward
through the doleful, overhanging verdurous
for many a slow prolong.
Then, suddenly, we broke out
onto the grassy everlasting.
Bright that shined, with a snow-capped immense
distant and ever away.
Still, no indicative,
but on the third revolving,
perceived it was at last, clifflike and wrinkled, and gray,
just standing there
sufficient, adequate, satisfactory—
surrounded by five spotted awkwards
and eight psoriatics,
and all these beneath
ravenous fecals circling in the blue.

Russell Streur

BICYCLE NUMBER NINE

That guy
Pedaling his bicycle
Wednesday morning
On Haynes Bridge Road
Could be any
Joe or maybe Jane
Just off of the boat
Joan hearing voices
Doe on a Trek
In the dark before dawn
He or maybe she
Is up early
Taking the Alpines by stages
A Mohammed in yellow
Ahead of the pack
The Helen on wheels
Heading downhill
Without any brakes
Some Che on a Schwinn
Off to the races
An anonymous smith
Out for a spin
Who's been riding in circles
Like the rest of the sages
All of these years
With a spoke or two missing
And a hole in the head
Through which
All the light in the world
Is going to spill
Any
Minute
Now.

Christine Swint

THE RED WEAVER
After Remedios Varo

In a corner of a dark room she winds
        a skein of rose-colored wool into a ball.
                Behind her graying crown of braids
fleur-de-lis on papered walls
        reflect their vague faces in the mirror,
                and from the open window—
fresh cut grass, lavender, sweet basil
        pale evening sun, breezes.
                She breathes in the clear light
of being and shuts her eyes.
        She dreams the red scarf she will knit
                has gathered itself from her lap
and become a woman. Rose-colored hair,
        arms open like wings—poised to fly under the sash.
                She wakes in her chair, wonders where
the scarf woman has flown.
        The light in the room has faded.
                Yarn rubs across her fingers.
She casts on the first row.
        Through the glass, onto rose-colored walls
                shadows and sunset shift like flames.

Marianne Szlyk

JUST A CLOSER WALK WITH THEE
after a video by Wycliffe Gordon

The trombone crawls
through the air
the way we crawl
through humidity
inside or out-
side, the drumbeat marking
off our steps.
We could be in a funeral
procession.
We could simply
be walking
from the car to
our work or Walmart
or our townhouse.

Just a closer walk with thee.
I know I will die
in summer,
bad air pressing down
on my chest
like the hands of a fat man
like the Salem ministers' stones
as I pray to my
Northern God
and his Mother Mary,
the Irishwoman
who wears
long sleeves in summer.

Perhaps if I had grown up
in this place,
I'd step out perkily
from the car's icy, edgy air
to the quick embrace of summer
to corporate chill.
This slow trombone, its music,

would be the sound
of evenings on the interstate
driving through dusk
and into the night
ticking off all the places
on my list.

Alice Teeter

THIS QUIET LAKE

There is a place where my sea meets your land,
or maybe it is your ocean meets my shore.
The luxurious waves can pick us up and lift us,
that pulsing salt water filling every pore,
the undulation of the swell as it travels
over sand bars and hillocks beneath,
rolling high up onto the warm beach to rest,
seaweed entwined, baking in hot sun on the sand.

But the hidden reef can cut our skin to tatters,
leave red clouds to swirl and mix in the surf,
rip tides can snatch us from the safety of the beach,
carry us far out, exhausted, to the lingering sharks,
a surge can pick us up, head straight inland for miles,
leave us stranded among strangers, gasping for breath.

I have traveled miles to find this quiet lake.
To this place where I now invite you to meet me.
It's a small body of water surrounded by color,
where large men walk with little white dogs,
and tiny children swim in high summer's heat.

This time of year, the breeze brings
showers of gold and red as you walk.
The wind comes down on the surface
of the water and murmurs kind words.

Sometimes you see a blue heron take off
and fly over a surface that is still as glass.
The bird glides over itself, wings outspread,
two worlds at once living and breathing –
the sky, the clouds, the shore
double in that flight.

Jessica Temple

BEARING

My favorite part of baking is before:
the batter dripping from the paddle,
or the yeasty dome rising in the metal bowl.

•

Last week my aunt called to tell me
it's alright that I'm not pregnant.
I started to think maybe it's not.

•

Once, as warning, grandmother told us about
her first husband – married because they had to.
Miscarried after a fall. Said she'd *prayed* for it.

•

One of those summers when heat
came early, a goat returned from the woods
with only one newborn. From the bulge

her belly had been, I knew that she
should've had two. I found the missing
by smell, just far enough in to stay shaded.

When I came back from shoveling,
it was already just a mound of fur,
wriggling as maggots danced inside.

•

My youngest sister asks me for recipes,
help with grammar. And when her doctor
said the pregnancy wasn't viable

she called me first, disquieted.
I could not say to her *This
is how to lose your baby.*

•

Both my sisters now busy themselves
with the making of people. I've seen
the work of it, the pulling back

from the edge. One kept it covered
for months – hidden like shirt-stays
under starched white trousers.

My nephews will be born
in Indian summer. One
will have dark skin, dark hair.

The other will be fair and
fearless. Both will grow tall.
They will not look like me.

Patricia Percival Thomas

WAITING FOR THE GOOD HUMOR MAN

Prone beneath mimosas,
the picture-book God
of rules and hellfire
deferred to the grace
of the natural world.
Pompons rained on me,
already dazed
by the scent of heat
rising off asphalt,
the smell visible
as a mirage
in a foreign legion film.

And though I don't believe
my catechism, as I did then,
I've kept my eyes open to visions,
mild thunderbolts which saints
might call the voice of God:
After a storm, starfish
littered the beach at Sanibel,
hundreds of six-armed bodies
expelled from the deep.
And fifty years ago, I saw
lilies of the valley emerge,
pristine, from the charnel
of rotten leaves.

Jeanie Thompson

ENRICO CARUSO REMEMBERS HELEN KELLER

*1918. The Georgian Terrance Hotel, Atlanta. Interior. Day.
Caruso, speaking, as if to no one.*

I tell you, I have recorded this voice on wax,
have let scientists explore my throat
searching for the lyric tenor's throbbing birdsong,
but never felt a soul enter as you did
when those keen fingers hovered on my lips, and
my breath, vibrato inscribed them. I swear the whirls
of your fingertips would play back the aria
if a needle could set their grooves.
Vois ma misere, helas. See my misery, alas,
all analogy fails me –
I am just a man who interprets song,
gives breath to notes, life to words –
but when I held your strong wrist,
your pulse at my lips, I knew an audience
with God –
Afterwards, I turned away, couldn't catch my breath.
(Had you taken it?) I know you swooned.
No applause, no *Bravo! Bravo!*
will touch me again as you did –
I have sung the best for you in my life, Helen Keller.

Natasha Trethewey

CARPENTER BEE

All winter long I have passed
beneath her nest—a hole no bigger
than the tip of my thumb.

Last year, before I was here,
she burrowed into the wood
framing my porch, drilled a network

of tunnels, her round body sturdy
for the work of building. Torpid
the cold months, she now pulls herself

out into the first warm days of spring
to tread the air outside my screen door,
floating in pure sunlight, humming

against a backdrop of green. She too
must smell the wisteria, see
—with her hundreds of eyes—purple

blossoms lacing the trees. Flower-
hopping she draws invisible lines,
the geometry of her flight. Drunk

on nectar, she can still find her way
back; though now she must be
confused, disoriented, doubting even

her own homing instinct—this beeline,
now, to nowhere. Today, the workmen
have come, plugged the hole—her threshold—

covered it with thick white paint, a scent
acrid and unfamiliar. She keeps hovering,
buzzing around the spot. Watching her,

I think of what I've left behind, returned to,
only to find everything changed, nothing but
my memory intact—like her eggs, still inside,

each in its separate cell—snug, ordered, certain.

Memye Curtis Tucker

GHOSTS

The ghosts of my grandmothers
will not be trifled with
or teased into speech—
they have already spoken. Now they watch.

Wax in the proper places,
smiles, sacrifice, no salt on silver,
children warned of the undertow,
a glass of milk for the stranger at the door,
as little lying as possible, as little truth—

they want such things remembered
and no jot or tittle more—
no sniveling *early to bed, waste not*—
they are awake all night,
they wasted nothing
and still want everything.

I try to satisfy them.
But I spill the milk, grow weary,
tell strangers
what I suspect of the truth.

Yet I speak with their voices,
lie under their quilts,
bear their hand-me-down names.

No man owns us,
but we own each other:
our lives are one long life,

milk, child, myth—
on good days
bequeathed like family silver.

I polish the spoons,
holding them up to the dark.

Dan Veach

VALE OF SOLES

The path along Peachtree Creek is soft
and sandy in the springtime. Filtered sun
brings out the blonde color, and the tracks
of shoe sole hieroglyphics written there—
myriad patterns, as different as fingerprints
diffract the light. I add mine to the mix, a palimpsest
that rubber soles rub out and write anew.

Some are cheap old sneakers,
some sleek running shoes. They're all
about the same at what they do—
give us some traction in the sand,
help us to hold our ground.

Keats could have used
a pair of these, to write his name
if not on water, then at least
upon these not so lone and level sands.
Pious folks ask, What would Jesus do?
I'd rather ponder, What would Keats
have worn? I'll bet,

the cheapest, plainest sneaker he could get—
black canvas with white rubber soles.
The name would appeal to him: *Converse*,
for *conversation*, for doing the exact *reverse*
of what most people do.

For chasing nightingales, they'd work as well
as some designer shoe, expensive, hip.
Money won't buy you a perfect purchase here,
as poets have always said, for what it's worth.
Sooner or later, our soles
always lose their grip.
Sooner or later, we all
slip and fall off the earth.

Sharon Venezio

POEM IN FAVOR OF DRIVING

In the dream I am happy
to be driving away from you,
from the nothing that we were.

In the dream the road hums
like a field of opium poppies.

There's an emptying of self
in the movement of the road,
a constant turning.

For 33 hours
from New Jersey
to Key West

sleeping in the back seat
somewhere in Georgia
under more stars
than I'd ever seen.

When I arrive
I descend 40 feet
into the ocean

explore an old sunken boat
its history
now coral and algae.

I feel the earth's axis
shift
into balance.

The ocean is always satisfied
after a storm,
each wave an elegy
for the world.

When I surface
I am happy
to be empty.

J. Phillip Walker

ELEGY IN THE COLLAPSE OF A BEAUTIFUL STRUCTURE

Someone said that this place—
a hogpen that became a granary
that became a garage and a fortress
of our childhood solitude—
went up like a temple,
the work divine and vital,
as if it were not just rendered from your vision,
but a part of *you* we could look to
and remember.

Now, decades later, the shell of the place resembles
something of the emptied pecan hulls, scatter-cast,
uncollected for years.
If we look carefully, we might discover an old pouch
of tobacco chew stowed in these cinderblock walls
and know it was you who left it, as if to remind us
of a responsibility you couldn't have known
would take us so long to realize. Excavated,
this reliquary would be empty, of course, but we
would open it anyway, letting the piquant smells escape,
the aromas of work and love and, well,
you, wash over us one last time, whispering
grandfather to our callow, heartsick ears.

This place seems all that is left of you.
It stands before us now, the deep-well water
at the faucet still rising from the black, fecund earth
tasting as chill and sweet as it did so long ago
with you there, watching the exertion of youth
wring us dry as cotton bolls in early winter;
the uneven concrete foundation wavy
like soft sand beneath crawdads scurrying
in the shallow creek close by; the roof punctured
by time, eroded by harsh rains leaving rust
in rashes all along the poor-pitched slope—

all of this still you, not yet gone,
waiting to be again.

Sue Walker

THREADS OUT OF THE BODY
After James Dickey

moments in Georgia,
in flickers of grace,
in chains of words
coiling-uncoiling
like snakes

       under a palmetto
       or in reeds
          waiting
       in a crisscross
       of twig-light

to true up
seasons of life
with the raggedness
of earth:
          sextants
    octants,
the complex star-angled keys
to everything.

William Walsh

OUTSIDE WINN DIXIE IN SUBURBAN PLAZA

Late Saturday night, 1986, and again I had no one
to hang out with, just a few poems
and a notion of what to do, when I saw a girl
not much older than sixteen in the back of a car
under the drunken parking lot lights,
her eyes watered-down with a slacked milky glaze,
full of what I knew was her childhood
being pushed off a north Georgia cliff by two boys
running into the Winn Dixie for more P.B.R.

After more than twenty years, I like to think I've helped
enough people along the way to quiet my regret,
repair the heavy elegy I carry on my back
for my father
and what he might say, "Never leave a stranger stranded."

As I walk through my house, I check the locks
on each door, turn off the lights, the t.v., the gas logs,
then up stairs to the hall and around the Legos
left on the floor. I step lightly to my children's room,
place a train on the dresser, adjust the bed covers,
tuck a bear under an arm, turn off a closet light.

Each cheek is dry to my kiss.
Room to room, I make my rounds
like a doctor or maybe like Superman
spinning the earth backwards to save Lois Lane.

Theresa Welford

THE BRIDE

My feet are killing me, she said,
and she pulled off her pumps
and left them in a corner,
just outside the social hall kitchen.
And there they stayed, obedient, side-by-side.
She whirled around the room, giggling,
apologizing for her bare feet, posing for snapshots.

She hugged the ladies fancied up in their best dresses,
their hair reflected in the lavender, pink, blue flowers.
They pressed their coral lips against her cheeks,
leaving prints, face powder, old-lady perfume.

She hugged the elderly gentlemen who were packed,
red-faced and sweating, into their Sunday suits.
They probably wished they could be outside on the front steps,
talking, smoking, coughing, laughing, wheezing.
They were good people.

Everywhere, kids were shrieking, chasing each other,
ducking behind the dark upright pianos.
She went after them, and she smiled over at me,
her satin skirt hiked up, just a little. Just enough.
Her ankles: I always told her how beautiful they were.

I was working my way around the room, too,
with one eye on the clock.
Not long before we'd take off for the honeymoon.
What a silly word.

Get a bunch of small-town Southern Baptists together,
and you know exactly what to expect:
We pray the Lord will bless your marriage. . . .
May God give you many long years together. . .
You lovebirds had better stay
on the straight and narrow tonight, you hear?!
Don't do anything I wouldn't do –

Where is she, by the way?
You reckon she's up and left?

When no one was looking, she slipped
into a Sunday School room
and closed the door behind her.
She choked to death.
On a little sandwich.
A *finger* sandwich, they call it.
Another silly word.
The doctor said it looked to him
like she started choking and went in there
because she didn't want to make a scene.

What was she thinking?
She's the only one who knows,
and she's not talking.
She was a *nurse*, for God's sake.
And by the way, God, what were *you* up to?
Answering someone's prayer
for a good parking space?

When I saw her gown, draped around her
on the linoleum floor, with those beautiful ankles
peeking out, my friends had to hold me up.

A week after the funeral, I sold my car.
Until we could afford a down payment,
it was going to be *our* car.
My best man and the other guys
tried to scrub it clean,
but it didn't work.
Their bawdy wedding-night jokes,
scrawled in white shoe-polish,
still scarred the paint.

Jennifer Wheelock

THE CONVERSATION TURNS TO WIDE-MOUTHED JARS

Thick Georgia air tongues
the huge hibiscus, a pink plate. We eat
pie on the back porch, ice cream melting
into crevices of crust. Mom and her sister
debate the merits of Rome versus
Granny Smith, half-runners and shellies,
Ball jars or Mason. "It's gotten awful hard to find
the wide-mouthed Masons." Mom rocks forward
three times in the slider, rises, shuffles
toward the shelves as I chase
her with a cane. She shoos it
like a fly, grabs a quart
of canned green beans and holds it out.
"See all these shellies." The jar trembles,
its weight causing an earthquake
along the length of her pale arm.
The beans in their liquid glisten
in late day light. Until now counting
bricks around the door frame—
his lips moving *two three four*—
Dad turns, squints, and points
at the jar. "My daddy made
moonshine and kept it in those jars.
When he died, I found him in the saw pit
beside an empty one."

Carey Scott Wilkerson

THIS IS ONLY A TEST

> *Critics have contended that the machine [the CERN Hadron Particle Accelerator] could produce a black hole that could eat the Earth or something equally catastrophic.* – New York Times

Let me see if I understand this:
Just outside Geneva, in a land of neutral zones,
scientists and pretenders to science are
contemplating a particle collision experiment
that some believe could open a black hole and end the world:
cascading protons, shot in opposite directions
at ninety-nine percent of the speed of light
around a giant, underground, internationally-funded electronic doughnut zero.

So, certain things are infinite, I suppose, and others last
what, a trillionth of a second(?), the length of time
they are measuring in Switzerland, staging that instant after the Big Bang.
And it turns out that part of the machine is actually in France,
which gives me hope.
The truth is I want to trust the romance of a visionary madness,
 to look past the apocalyptic overtones—because that's what I do– and toward
a myth, a dream of revelation, a quantum state of insight.

To prepare for this, I might recall Icarus plummeting from
some unimaginable height, his wings melted not so much
by the heat of Apollo's flaming chariot as, rather,
by the light of close scrutiny, of observable facts,
or by the received view that humans should not fly.
Perhaps it is a consolation to find, in all those black-and-white film clips
of absurdly improbable, planes flapping, gyrating, churning, twirling, some
argument for the failure of any rational enterprise.
And one could do worse than to end up in a Breugel painting,
each day, dressing up for the same lyrical end, replaying, repeating,
returning round again, to the limits of philosophy and Flemmish high culture,
that moment when it all went wrong.

Like so much else, the Hadron Collider's properly working mechanism
is a question of temperature regulation.

One is warned never to burn bridges, either real or metaphorical.
Keeping one's cool is a first principle in polite company.
And it is basic to our shared experience
that an overcooked egg becomes an art installation.
Einstein, an American émigré, won the Nobel Prize not for his work on relativity,
but for a study of the photoelectric effect, a study of light, of heat.

Every time I burn my fingers changing a light-bulb, it occurs to me that–
because sixty-watts of light produce seventy-seven degrees of ambient radiation,
two-hundred sixty degrees of surface radiant heat,
nd over four-thousand at its vacuum core–illumination is morally ambiguous.
Thus are we known to be characteristically ambivalent about Good and Evil
but fastidious on the question of Hot and Cold.

At some point, someone, presumably, must turn the machine on,
a gesture of anticipatory grace, nostrums sweeping over the altar,
an entire aesthetic of desire held in flux in the circumference of
a colossal zero buried under the cathedrals of ancient Europa.
If we are to glimpse something numinous lost to numerical
puzzles, taking up the timeline in a coil around the hand, under the elbow,
the cosmological extension cord put away, then I want to see what Icarus sees
in the instant just after his wings dissolve but before he falls.
I want to record the discipline of sixteenth century paint and Greek fantasy;
a family of many artists, and Pieter Bruegel the Elder who
signed his work with a misspelling of his own name.

At the sub-atomic level, I am watching myself composing my signature,
the lurid and unseemly continuity of letters flowing out
of themselves, into the encoded space of a blank page.
I see unmappable shorelines of identity looping endlessly
around the alphabet, reeling through catalogs of imperfectly
dotted i's, blind concessions to fate over and over without irony,
the vague memory of breakfast with a stranger under a hastily scribbled sun or
telephone doodles dutifully retraced,
forever if necessary,
until I get it right.

M. L. Williams

SUMMER THUNDERSTORM

Sunshine around the clouds doles no comfort. Nimbus mushrooms—I want to say atomic—rises spreads, blossoms like roses on old Disney shows Sunday nights before cold war bedtime. Rains through the shine and they say around here the devil's beating his wife. They say around here y'all are welcome honey or that neighborhood is mixed. Smothered and covered. Will wash it out and the lightning cracks through, terrible light. Terrible light. Burn leaf piles and ropes of smoke trouble oak branches. We don't talk about that. Loud when it breaks but it cools and the roads steam and the ditches run. Bless your heart they say.

Patricia Williams

EVERYTHING USEFUL I KNOW ABOUT LIFE I LEARNED FROM MARGARET MITCHELL

The first time I read *Gone with the Wind*
I was just past fourteen —

checked it out over Christmas vacation,
read it every school year thereafter.
America's second favorite book —

it was my Bible.

    Margaret's tale tells of survival —

    a world of century-old oaks,
    ripening cotton, stately white columns,
    how it imploded —

    some came through, others went under;
    ants, drowning in sweetness.

Scarlett, the belle, had 'gumption' —

able to revise, innovate,
loosen corseting social stays,
dress in green velvet curtains —

unable to handle passion
that trapped and entangled.

    Margaret wrote of suffering —

    of unyielding structures,
    change in convention;
    insecurity, uncertainty;
    a saga of surrender, rebellion —

    an unresolved scene, left for tomorrow.

Austin Wilson

TREMBLING EARTH

                  Walking on what seems an island
in the swamp,
          "the land of trembling earth,"
    what *Okefenokee* means in the Creek spoken by the Seminoles,
      you make the ground shiver
                  with each tentative step,
       the peat bog as shaky as a faultline
           though the quaking earth moves only a little.

You sink into what feels like a sponge
        and then step out of a footprint filling with water.

      It is not the quicksand that the moviemakers loved to film,
          quicksand they made themselves with
              sawdust and water back on higher ground
      where they could dig a hole, like at Trader's Hill or near
          High Bluff Primitive Baptist Church, where
            old Swampers were buried, a place where
a grave wouldn't float a coffin,
      where gators wouldn't turn a burial ground
          into a den.

               The swamp was where my father
took me, before the boardwalks, the observation towers, the boat tours,
      the wildlife shows of milking rattlers, men wrestling alligators,
and the black bears chained to stakes
           before there was a Swamp Park, a Refuge.

He put me out of the boat and made me walk on ground
      that shook, that pulled you down, that seemed ready to leave you
        without anything to stand on,

      as if to show me that the way things were at home
          was natural, the way the world was.

Linda Wimberly

YOUR VOICE SURPRISED ME

Rising out of parched pages,
it soared
above the drowsy nod of drone.

Of course I couldn't see you,
but I could hang every word
on a narrow line, suspend them
above the dusty floor
and watch while they danced
on staccato beats.

Or I could take the words
down a minor scale
and listen as your voice descended
into a midnight kind of blue.

Your voice surprised me.
As I listened,
it wasn't hard
to follow you
into a darkened room
and close the door.

Pete Wingard

MOTHER USED ONLY PAPER NAPKINS

Look at all the animals in the wild
with no worry of livelihood.
Jesus' little birdies.

With neighbors
from block after block of salt-box houses
we file out in the dark of morning
our headlights like miner's lamps.
We work to fill the weekend shopping carts
(gleaming tic-tac-toe boards on wheels)
with pegs for our whack-a-mole lives. With evening
we are dirty with mission statements, eyes blurred
from deadlines, backs bent from shoring paper
overhead. A number, with a comma
and two decimal places as small
as bits of cotton fiber in a banknote
is our existence as we stretch
to tack on one more digit
exactly to the left of life.

Like rows of farmed pines
flicking past an open window
each row planted exactly
so many feet apart
and growing straight and tall
toward its own small patch
of fleeting blue, our shriveled limbs
must be kept to ourselves in acre after acre
of civilized forest.

Growing up
I can't ever remember an occasion
with linen napkins.
Everything was peeled apart, balled up
then thrown away.
The sun came up in one window
and went down in the other.

Repeated.

Crystal Woods

ON MONDRIAN'S GRAVE
Brooklyn, New York

On the Metro, block after block
in rocking darkness, stepping off
at Cypress Hills Cemetery into grass
that grows in the shadow of his name.
Certainly he smiles at this, green now
after so much posturing.

Crosslegged, I cue up boogie woogie,
one earbud for me, the other dangling earthward
to stir his finger bones scattered now
like lengths of broken chalk. But once
those hands formed red, blue, yellow tiles
on black grids straight and sharp
as the creases in his suit pants. He listed home
his first New York evening
drunk on jazz and neon, not a Nazi in sight.

Months later, as pneumonia raged,
he became his own work:
coughing blood, pallor cyanotic
under yellow lights in that white studio,
no better abstraction than death.

William Wright

GRIEF MAP

Dodd Hopkins lost his mind the day after his wife passed,
left his bed hours before the sun tipped the mountain's edge.
The morning wind was to his ear a prophetic tongue.

In sleeping clothes, barefoot, the moon's scant flame to light
his way, he walked into woods over briars and bramble
fully numb, wandered until dawn dipped the sky

in blue. He gathered all the flowers he could find, made
trips back and forth from woods to home with armfuls
of fringed phacelia, trillium, gentian, trailing arbutus.

The land's unsteady gable dizzied him, and, near noon,
his feet bleeding and the solar bath of light singeing his skin,
his brain absorbed the rate at which Earth spun.

He knew that no alchemies would summon
her, that no mix of ivy and thorn and blood would stall
the devils that carved the last of his sense away. He couldn't

shake the vision of her body underground, bleeding dry.
So he reaped and reaped until he felt satisfied he'd upset
spring's dark womb, made a hex of its design, and for weeks

more crept the ridges in mourning, snatching plants up
by fistfuls, his only solace the fibrous sounds of tearing taproot,
his smile the raveling of that embroidery.

He filled the house with her—blooms and leaves
took the shape her body had pressed into their bed. Nights
he cooked for two, placed wild onion and daffodils

in her supper chair. He lined apple leaves along the window
sills she used to crack to let the warmer seasons in.
Once he'd finished with the house, he transcribed her

into the winding path she'd tread in grass and mud
to tend their yard, to feed the garden until it fed them back.
And though all this work summoned her once or twice

to shimmer in his dreams, these steeped floras made the map
of grief he traveled every day, toiled to tend, even as all
he did to keep her there wilted, cracked, or blew away.

Kevin Young

WHOLE HOG
In Memoriam Jake Adam York

It is heavy,
a hog, you need
to stay

up all night, nursing
the fire like a beer,
or rise early

like we did, that first time
you taught me how
to drag December

awake into flame,
lighting pecan
& hickory, passed

between cinder block
& ash. Do you dig
a pit? No,

we build one
last house
for the huge sow

who we know
rooted & ranged
the given ground.

Head on, scrubbed, split,
the pig's skin
crackles, a communion

of it—no spit,
just shoveling coals
like a locomotive

engineer, boilerman,
rounder—
Casey Jones

mounted to his cabin
& he took his farewell
trip to the promised land—

the smoke everywhere
like a prayer, clinging
your clothes for days

we do not wish
to wash away. To share
the weight, to wear it—

to honor the creature
by devouring it
whole—we know she

would return
the favor. *He looked*
at his watch

& his watch
was slow. Steam rises sweet
among the maples

& bamboo. How
do you know
it is done? The hog

will tell you.

Andrew Zawacki

GEORGIA

I don't sleep Georgia
I shoot bullets into the dark
the blunt mimeographic dark
the middle dark Georgia
outside the outside
whatever a ghost's front tooth is Georgia
let alone ballistics
whatever pulls back the hammer Georgia
coughing up sulfur and strobes of negate
I wait Georgia
think Georgia
the fire is like the snow Georgia
the snow wipes out a oneway street puts nothing in its place
snow is not like the snow Georgia
one is theorem the other will thaw
night is the neighbor girl
she hangs her laundry
she sits on the step
the leaves on the tree in her yard are like florins
her sliding door dress in a squall Georgia
her flowers what is a flower Georgia
a trace what is trace
I listen to the noises every last one Georgia
I love every last noise on the violet fields
they bicker and click
the clamors I mean
blur as if struck with a Lucifer match
guesswork Georgia
netherlight's joke
I see smoke it rises it quadrilles Georgia
tungsten Georgia
sliver tongued
the smoke is a little less smoke in the air
little by little Georgia
it comes to that
not even Georgia
I walk wolfstep into the shadow Georgia
the nodding orchestral branches

shellacked as if a fountain turned and forced its gravity turn
the skuzzy drag queen dawn Georgia
hours away from hours away
a motor idles
reverse in the drive
tromp-l'œil frisking the shrubbery Georgia
the high beams taper the porch lamp expires
I take out the garbage Georgia
will it rain or snow
will the weather Georgia
the winter here is not your winter
it's pixeled it's *chien et loup* Georgia
a dumdum blank to the clavicle Georgia
assassin crouched at the front of the house assassin waiting in back
I don't give a shit Georgia
difference itself can differ Georgia
and everything's different now
I buried a friend far away Georgia
in France Georgia
it wasn't funny Georgia
we sat at a table I kissed him goodbye he turned around never came back
maybe you already heard it Georgia
I'm tired of talking about it
that was then and this is then and not even Georgia not even
I listen Georgia
to the racket the clatter
the clangors clang if you hearken Georgia
and that noise makes a noise if you
a peloton of din Georgia
you have to sonar yourself
The question of is is is it Georgia
the ranges are thrift store crinoline Georgia
the stars are of mescal
casbahs of tin
flayed what is it to flay something Georgia
mountains unplugged the moon flipped off
if music is cleaved from a flower Georgia
if music cleaves to the flower Georgia
liveforever and purple clover
but nothing lives that long Georgia
or even half that long
All things that are are unlit Georgia
black like lapis in a quitted room
the feedback Georgia

the anvil's hymnal
a dial-tone looped in a flophouse Georgia
an explosive packed in a microchip
petals of 0 petals of 1
rips a hole of a fractal dimension
shrapnel Georgia
collateral damage
call it what you will
Here is the road the outskirts Georgia
here is a city
is the same city
and I don't know this city Georgia
and I don't know if I want to know
what is it that anyone knows Georgia
really Georgia
in the end Georgia
Some say your eyes are charcoal Georgia
some say siren some djinn
I don't say Georgia
it isn't for me
I don't have a bone in my body
the unquick have a habit of loitering Georgia
a bad one I willn't say otherwise
it seems to get them through alright
don't know what they see in it
as if they're awake what is wakefulness Georgia
with the silencer on what is silence Georgia
someone around here will know Georgia
somebody ought to know something
The house next door has gone tattletale gray
its chimney a jigsaw of mortar and frost
threadbare nay barren
crash tested Georgia
rapunzeling up on a fidgety draft
the pine straw to flicker and parry
and the eglantine to wither Georgia
and snowflakes tatter the shutters Georgia
like flak from a showdown in Kelvin air
"*L'attente commence quand il n'y a…*" Georgia
"*…plus rien à attendre, ni même la fin de l'attente*"
that nothing come between us Georgia
but me
and you
and the hollow between

I prune your buds
unbutton my ribs
pot you inside like a bonsai Georgia
buddha napping in tiny shade
buddha at rest with an almsgiving bowl
it's aliment vs. ailment Georgia
I won't let you go it alone
you and your poor man's briar patch
and your ne'er-do-well well well
Heat lightning daubs the collodion hills
and a howling
and how close
how close to the bone does it get Georgia
do you pull its pin with a cinch of the jaw
pulver its craw with a flinch of the fist
I hurry here is the wind
and cold the inaudible decibel
the irises flushed in saffron
in bayonet red
in cymbeline
no clean angle
simulacra Georgia
everything's dirty and doubled Georgia
I say
you can try to break it it will break you
I say
everything is breakable Georgia
melody Georgia
melt water
a pressure a femur a fever a wife
syllables virused by syllables Georgia
the bicycle is
the memory card is
the brackish canal where a boat is Georgia
and the boat and where is it headed Georgia
the tanzanite dew of your nerve endings
cuts me keeps me alert
I unlatch the window
it sticks Georgia
sometimes I see past the paint flecks Georgia
and sometimes the pane is the object I see
and sometime come a whirring Georgia
like an alabaster lung Georgia
a valentine stitched in Kevlar Georgia

blown in Venetian glass
it's beautiful Georgia
that's one word Georgia
like a landslide
like a negligée
carnelian Georgia
an impasse's path
the glass in the garden is bulletproof
but our bodies are not of glass Georgia
let's bloom Georgia
this popstand
this podunk five and dime a dozen
our brains all over the passenger seat
our underwear on the dash
desire from the formal idea thereof
I
is a shotgun shell Georgia
imma – and imminent
the image as such
your quidditas throws a wrench in the work
but this engine runs on wrenches Georgia
anti-freeze and no egress Georgia
parousia stalled in a parking lot
the phenomenon's faulty ignition
you're alasless Georgia
harassless Georgia
from your slackass jeans to your Jesus Georgia
ersatz and aliased
lacking alack
sans any essence or pretense of presence
you're leeward Georgia
a bejeweled word Georgia
and fuck you anyway
vowellewd Georgia
face card missing a face Georgia
they're dead Georgia
I said they were dead
I didn't say they weren't dancing
The clouds are low they will tumble down Georgia
I spread my arms they get tired Georgia
to catch them Georgia
from shattering Georgia
my eyes they get tired I don't shut them Georgia
it's like this Georgia

unlike this Georgia
between the bed and the kitchen Georgia
one plate and another
one fag and another
the ashtray the butane lighter Georgia
an ice cube and its plastic cell
a pill and the pillow
whetstone and knife
one bag of coffee one packet of creamer an orange a slice of bread
between the door and the hinge Georgia
the razor blades and the bathtub Georgia
a forest of goneness a windrow of kindling a forge nail hidden in grass
I don't cry Georgia
you know what they say
whoever the they is who say what they say
but I was never real Georgia
but the hell if I know what is
I'm a scarecrow Georgia
a voodoo doll
no for a left leg yes yes for my right it's calamity Georgia
flammable Georgia
periplum scribbled all over the board
a torso of origami folds
crease for an eyelash a Crayola head
with a watermark Georgia
80-gram
you roll it you lick it you drag on it Georgia
I don't say it ain't kitschy Georgia
like cotton candy
like holding hands
so you've had it up to here huh
there isn't a soul who don't have it to here
the android floral in cyanine Georgia
acacia version 2.0
the horizon a linen of spilled anjou
of lint and candle wax
I call Georgia
my voice shot Georgia
parasites sur la ligne Georgia
the flowers rattle
I 'listen the flowers'
and the I I am is that ruckus Georgia
it's pretty Georgia
that's a word comes to mind

a punkass word
but a word all the same
an adjective out of bric-a-brac
we let it return to its querulous hive
"a heaven of stones whose / swiftness…" Georgia
"…made their separate orbits / one, that slackening would fall"
I call out Georgia
because that you
because that you are whatever Georgia
but it's dint Georgia
Teflon Georgia
polycarbonate it opens on impact Georgia
beryl raised to the second power with the safety off and the trigger rigged
I don't knock Georgia
my brass knuckles buffed
with a rough like liquid oxygen and a pilot light and a fraying fuse
it's sugar Georgia
burnt Georgia
pure cane Georgia and maybe baby you're
nothing more than synecdoche Georgia
a piece of a shred of a shard of a frag-
you're blitzkrieg Georgia
don't 'lady' me Georgia
I've got theremin lacing the bloodstream George
and a spinning roulette for a ticker George
a slug cocked snug in the six-shooter chamber
a 16.6% chance
You're a bitch Georgia
a drill bit
by me I mean third-person plural Georgia
a lake effect Georgia
all haggardlike Georgia
a hangman Georgia
a hanged man Georgia
here's a lullaby Georgia
with geraniums Georgia
there there Georgia
no there there Georgia
and may your dreams be couturier sewn
in pinafores and dainty furbelow
It's not the same midnight threnody
that 3 in the morning laments
an asthmatic wheeze in the lavender Georgia
a powwow of bats in the arbor Georgia

aurora borealis Georgia
haint blue
and barleycorn bluish and pollen do powder the sill Georgia
'n' still Georgia
"The first snow was a white sand
that made the white rocks seem red"
hence I wed Georgia
the roof with the ladder
lean out to inquire of the distance
there's a lot to be learned by leaning Georgia
I can't put a number to it
nothing that matters is numbered Georgia
if anything can truly be said to
plaster cast and splint Georgia
weeds that whisker a cracking quoin
lachryma Georgia
the spigot leaking
laid thee down by the waters and wept
the driveway tailored in crepe Georgia
I swept it of leaves the leaves didn't stay
I swept it of bluster the gust did not stay
my scarce understanding of oak didn't stay
nor knowledge of climate
nor knowledge of season
dampness didn't
and dryness didn't
and I didn't stay there myself Georgia
any old thing can unsolder a moment
nearly everything does
erosion is a simple name for it Georgia
but it hides other themes that are hard
like a noun it takes the place of a thing
but doesn't kill it off
it shackles the signified to a stump
then chucks the log in the crick
a facade Georgia
a fusillade
the firing squad and the wall Georgia
a cenotaph
in the aftermath
of petty Georgia
your petticoat slipping
pussy – and pistolwhipped son of a Georgia
if I ever

I swear if I
if you ever so much as hint at Georgia
I don't know what I'd fixin' to fix ya
know not what I would do
but no one's ever sure what they're capable of
so I try Georgia
I try to remit
this dragnet that dredges the ends of an earth
what is it Georgia
is it Georgia
or is it not
I can't figure it Georgia
'twon't stay in focus
it doesn't possess a center or an outside
or an in
I'd say
like skipping a stone and the shale doesn't sink
or taming a tidal wave with a riding crop
or swimming inside a prism Georgia
its J/psi particles and xanadus of jade
bladed among the tall vitrines of a gilt arcade in a country Georgia
fenestral Georgia
and fractured Georgia
and can't tell where your skin leaves off and the color begins to begin
like looking for midday at 2 of the
clock when your 5 o'clock
shadow is early
but truth is it isn't like anything Georgia
not like any anything
not even currents are so much surrounded
they can't be split one from the water
you can call it a fact of life if you like
but it's nothing to do with facticity Georgia
let alone with a life Georgia
let alone with someone else's life
I don't know Georgia
don't know what I don't
sleet the drizzle the banshee oblique
high-volt deadbolt barbwirespeak
and I'm damned if you do either Georgia
the both of us are damnation Georgia
a hawk owl perched on the larch's bough
and rot
"But a sudden piece of glass on a sidewalk" Georgia

"Or a nickel tune in a music box
A shadow on a wall at night
And I would remember"
or December beneath a kaleidoscope rain
a digital rain
la pluie numérique
a lukewarm rinse without downpour Georgia
velocity Georgia
lovely as luck
that shower kick up as a rustle Georgia
a madrigal solo
a hiss in the cedars
some scrape from out back like flintlock Georgia
on the wood pile
on the axe handle
dithers and zags like a swarm Georgia
dilly-
dally and para-
diddle
a gramophone needle's static Georgia
on the asphalt Georgia
the police station roof
a wet from up north in a weight from up north
like a secret swerving toward rumor Georgia
it lapses Georgia
collapses Georgia
and the shush it starts to divide Georgia
by square root
by willow root
it fractions in Fibonacci Georgia
like artillery Georgia
like friendly fire
by logarithm by analog
it unloads Georgia
the cargo it's schlepped
renders its ballast elastic Georgia
dilates Georgia
dilutes itself
flutes the ravine and the river gap Georgia
letterpressed Georgia
an accordion's chord
like the soggy crumbs of Hop o' My Thumb
or HTML from the stratosphere Georgia
in smithereens Georgia

alarm tripped Georgia
out the emergency exit marked Georgia
I draw a line in the gravelly sand
you draw a break in the line
it's not right Georgia
quasi-floozy
a kite panhandling the breeze Georgia
pinned to the sky like a wedding corsage
on a tie-dye concert tee
The trees stand gunmetal
steel in the storm
then crack like a rifle report
nobody sees it coming Georgia
at crepuscule
in the alkaline dusk
maybe that's half the excitement Georgia
you would know better
bitterer than I
my opium Georgia
with your feldsparring drawl
my slapstick and lipstick and stick 'em up Georgia
you twang Georgia
like a daisycutter
a radio transmitter's muttering dreck
I'm an echo playing bumper cars in basilicas of Georgia Georgia
a silhouette
I'm a satin flower
I'm a sick bag and the sick Georgia
an avalanche an insomniateque
a ruby-throated humming
from my throat if I had a throat Georgia
it's not unlike a kiddie cartoon
fluorescent way out of proportion Georgia
I see horses
running through diamonds Georgia I
can't hold
it all in my head
it's sad Georgia
like the word itself
I hesitate to use it
but sometimes another word won't do when a word is the one you want
you think Pierrot Georgia
like pirouette Georgia
dunno if the words are related

I know almost nothing of language Georgia
I care too much to care
I lie down on the couch
a few birds a small tremor
the wind is encoded to rustle the gowns of the trees
a chirp like spit bite acid Georgia
an injection Georgia
an infection Georgia
via authorized medical application of a sterilized syringe
I went
too far Georgia
not near far enough
like a switch on the fritz in a binary star
and the steering column is hotwired Georgia
and piss in the tank for petrol Georgia
listing hydraulic or limping on fumes
to seize the shore of your flash flooded cellar
before it unfastens the linoleum floor
I'm sorry Georgia
I'm not sorry Georgia
I don't mean a single word that issue forth from mine own mouth
"what lies / outside us…" Georgia "…is not formless, it's
as we are, the sound itself"
I've heard Georgia
on entering an unfamiliar room
a blind person locates the source of that sound
leaky faucet
a failing bulb
the refrigerator's drone
and orients her touch around this point
sometimes the sound is a second person
in which case community Georgia
at others the ear meets no obstacle
and one is unmoored in a dumbshow of one
overhearing the blood move around in the brain
centrifugal Georgia
inch by inch
the fulcrum permits a perimeter Georgia
like rings advancing radaresque in a pond where a pebble
snapped the surface
curve by corner by
lintel by latch
then ricochet Georgia
like noon off a gun

the exterior turns internal Georgia
a context caroms from the contours
and every border could not at first
be seen or felt to be
is now revealed as environment Georgia
to fetter the setting it occupies
and this becomes known as the world Georgia
or at least as one world
among possible worlds
however exhausted the term Georgia
in company or alone
and whether those possible worlds Georgia
be many
or only
my own
I call you Georgia
in the fissure of you
the flocked light and parataxis of you
are you going to come before the darkness shuck its dark
mercury Georgia
musket ball Georgia
unlessless Georgia
for the blossoms Georgia
the night is leaded with cheap perfume
I won't sleep Georgia
I'll wait up

for Sandrine

Rebecca Ziegler

SPRING COMES TO THE COASTAL PLAIN

On the coastal plain,
starting in February,
the flowers creep in.

Winter is just plain
ornery – just contrary
on the coastal plain.

Tricked by frequent rain,
and by warm February
days, flowers creep in.

Unwary blooms are slain
by frosts in February
on the coastal plain.

When, instead of rain,
there's sleet in February,
dead flowers creep in.

One day against the grain
chokes a flowering tree
on the coastal plain.

Still, the budding trees
bloom and sometimes freeze.
On February's coastal plain
the flowers creep in.

CONTRIBUTOR'S NOTES AND BIOGRAPHIES

SARA AMIS grew up in Ringgold, Georgia and holds a BA in Anthropology from Georgia State University and an MFA in Creative Writing from the University of Georgia. Her work has appeared in *Magpie Magazine, The Dead Mule School of Southern Literature, Jabberwocky 3* and *5, Datura, Lilith: Queen of the Desert, Moon Milk Review, Southern Fried Weirdness: Reconstruction, Right Hand Pointing, Luna Station Quarterly* and *The Moment of Change*, an anthology of feminist speculative poetry by Aqueduct Press. Her poem series *The Sophia Leaves Text Messages* was published as a hand-bound limited edition by Papaveria Press in 2009. She is a regular columnist for *Luna Station Quarterly* and *Patheos.com.*

DIANA ANHALT is the author of articles, book reviews and short stories published in both English and Spanish, as was her book, *A Gathering of Fugitives: American Political Expatriates in Mexico 1948-1965* (Archer Books). More recently, two of her chapbooks— *Second Skin* (Future Cycle Press) and, *Lives of Straw* (Finishing Line Press)—have been released. *The Atlanta Review, Nimrod, Comstock Review* and *Passager* are among the publications where her poetry has appeared.

KEITH BADOWSKI is a co-founder and editor of Brick Road Poetry Press (Columbus, GA). His poetry has appeared in *FutureCycle Poetry, Birmingham Arts Journal, Monkey, Rambunctious Review,* and *Reach of Song.* His recent chapbook of spontaneous poetry is titled *My Wife Warned Me and I Did It Anyway.* He was the President of the Georgia Poetry Society, 2009-2010.

REBECCA BAGGOT has lived most of her life in Georgia, most recently in Athens, where she writes and works as an academic advisor for the Franklin College of Arts and Sciences at the University of Georgia. She is the author of four chapbooks, most recently *God Puts on the Body of a Deer* (Main Street Rag, 2010) and *Thalassa* (Finishing Line Press, 2011). Recent work has appeared in *Crab Orchard Review, New Letters, Southern Poetry Review,* and *Tar River Poetry.* "Alleluia" first appeared in *The Atlanta Review.*

SARA BAKER is a novelist, short story writer and poet. Her stories have been published in or are forthcoming in *The Examined Life, The Chattahoochee Review, The New Quarterly, The Spirit that Moves Us, The*

Habersham Review, and *The Lullwater Review*. Her poetry has appeared in *The 2011 Hippocrates Prize for Poetry and Medicine, The Healing Muse, Ars Medica, The Yale Journal of Humanities in Medicine, The Journal of Poetry Therapy* and elsewhere. Her chapbook, *Brancusi's Egg,* was published by *Finishing Line Press* in 2013. A radio play "A Wagner Matinee" was produced by NPR and BBC. She has written two novels, one of which was a finalist in the Hemingway Days first novel contest. Sara holds a Masters degree from Boston College. She has taught English at the University of Georgia, The Georgia Institute of Technology, and Piedmont College. Her own journey with chronic illness has led her to create the *Woven Dialog Workshops*, writing workshops that aid in facilitating the healing process.

MARCIA BARNES moved to Warner Robins, Georgia, in 2004, and wrote several short stories, two children's books, and published a heritage cookbook, *The Little Book of Secret Family Recipes,* in 2008. After moving to Hiawassee, Georgia, in 2009, her writing took a turn to research, and resulted in three years of study and writing about the mountains of Georgia, and the earliest missionaries, ministers, and settlers who pioneered the northeastern part of the state.

LAURA LEE BEASLEY recently completed her Ph.D. at Georgia State University where she worked as an assistant editor for *Five Points* and as the poetry editor for *New South*. Her poems have appeared in *Time You Let Me In*, an anthology edited by Naomi Shihab Nye, *the Texas Observer*, and the *Silk Road Review.*

PHILIP BELCHER is the Vice President of Programs for The Community Foundation of Western North Carolina in Asheville and the author of a chapbook, *The Flies and Their Lovely Names*, from Stepping Stones Press. A graduate of Furman University, Southeastern Baptist Theological Seminary, and the Duke University School of Law, he also has an MFA in Poetry from Converse College and is the recipient of the Porter Fleming Prize in Poetry. Belcher's poems and prose have appeared in numerous journals, including *Asheville Poetry Review, The Southeast Review, Shenandoah, 2River View, Southern Humanities Review, Passages North, Fugue, VPR,* and *The Southern Quarterly.*

WILL BLAIR holds an MA in English from the University of West Georgia. He is the editor of *Newnan/Coweta Magazine*, a supplement of The *Newnan Times-Herald* newspaper. A longtime community journalist and local writer, he has only recently undertaken poetry.

MARGARET BLAKE'S poems have appeared or are forthcoming in *The Southern Poetry Anthology, Volume V: Georgia, Tar River,* and *Slipstream*. She is currently engaged in a five-summer MFA program at Sewanee, the University of the South, and during the year, she teaches high school English in Atlanta.

DAVID BOTTOMS'S first book, *Shooting Rats at the Bibb County Dump*, was chosen by Robert Penn Warren as winner of the 1979 Walt Whitman Award of the Academy of American Poets. His poems have appeared widely in magazines such as *The New Yorker, The Atlantic, Harper's, Poetry,* and *The Paris Review*, as well as in sixty anthologies and textbooks. He is the author of seven other books of poetry, two novels, and a book of essays and interviews. His most recent book of poems, *We Almost Disappear*, was released in the fall of 2011. Among his other awards are the Frederick Bock Prize and the Levinson Prize, both from *Poetry* magazine, an Ingram Merrill Award, an Award in Literature from the American Academy and Institute of Arts and Letters, and fellowships from the National Endowment for the Arts and the John Simon Guggenheim Memorial Foundation. He has given readings at over 200 colleges and universities across the country, as well as the Guggenheim Museum, the Library of Congress, and the American Academy in Rome. He has served as the Richard Hugo Poet-in-Residence at the University of Montana, the Ferrol Sams Distinguished Writer at Mercer University, and the Chaffee Visiting Poet-in-Residence at Johns Hopkins University. He lives with his wife and daughter in Atlanta, where he holds the Amos Distinguished Chair in English Letters at Georgia State University. A book of essays on his work, *David Bottoms: Critical Essays and Interviews* edited by William Walsh, was published in 2010. He is the recipient of a 2011 Governor's Award in the Humanities, sponsored by the Georgia Humanities Council, and he served for twelve years as Poet Laureate of Georgia. "Under the Vulture-Tree" is from *Armored Hearts: Selected and New Poems*, Copper Canyon Press, 1985. "Eye to Eye" was published in the August 12 & 19, 2013 edition of The New Yorker.

DEBORAH BRANDON was born in Savannah and lived there until the age of eight. Her work has appeared in [PANK], *Bombay Gin, Mom Egg Review, Denver Quarterly, Moonshot, Cadillac Cicatrix, MiPoesias* and *Ocho Magazine* as well as in an anthology, *Writing the Walls Down*, from TransGenre Press. She holds an MFA in Writing from the School of the Art Institute of Chicago.

JODY BROOKS lives in Atlanta, GA. Her work has appeared recently in *DIAGRAM, The Florida Review, South Dakota Review, Hobart, KneeJerk,* and *Hot Metal Bridge*.

JENNY MARY BROWN'S work is either featured or forthcoming from *Berkeley Poetry Review, Tipton Poetry Journal, Sugar House, Hothouse Magazine,* and *Pale Horse.* She is a PhD candidate in English for Creative Writing – Poetry at Georgia State University. She is currently the art director at *District* and the Editor-in-Chief of *New South.* She lives in Little Five Points.

JERICHO BROWN is the recipient of fellowships from the Radcliffe Institute for Advanced Study at Harvard University and the National Endowment for the Arts. His poems have appeared or are forthcoming in journals and anthologies including, *Callaloo, The Nation, The New Yorker, Oxford American, The New Republic, 100 Best African American Poems, Ascent of Angles,* and *The Best American Poetry.* His first book, *Please,* won the American Book Award, and his second book, *The New Testament,* is forthcoming from Copper Canyon Press. Brown is currently an Assistant Professor at Emory University.

STACEY LYNN BROWN is a poet, playwright, and essayist from Atlanta, Georgia. Her work has appeared in numerous journals, including *Crab Orchard Review, Copper Nickel, The Volta, Barn Owl Review,* and *Southern Quarterly,* as well as the *From the Fishouse, Rumpus, Southern Poetry: Georgia,* and *Book of Scented Things* anthologies. She is the author of the book-length poem *Cradle Song* (C&R Press, 2009) and is the co-editor, with Oliver de la Paz, of *A Face to Meet the Faces: An Anthology of Contemporary Persona Poetry* (The University of Akron Press, 2012). She teaches creative writing at Indiana University in Bloomington.

KATHRYN STRIPLING BYER, a native of SW Georgia, served as NC's first woman Poet Laureate. Her work has appeared in numerous anthologies and journals, including *Atlantic Monthly, Poetry, Georgia Review, American Scholar,* and *Cortland Review.* Her first book, *The Girl in the Midst of the Harvest,* was an Associated Writing Programs finalist chosen by John F. Nims and published by Texas Tech U. Press. LSU Press has published subsequent books including *Wildwood Flower,* an Academy of American Poets Laughlin Selection. Her most recent book, *Descent,* received the NC Book Award for poetry. Her chapbook, *The Vishnu Bird,* is available from Wind Publications. She lives in the mountains of western North Carolina.

BRIGITTE BYRD is a French-American poet, author of three poetry books, including *Song of a Living Room* (Ahsahta Press). Her most recent work is featured in *Sentence 10* and *Solstice Lit,* and forthcoming in *Ampersand Review and Anvil Lit.* With a Ph. D. in English (Poetry as a Genre and Theory of Performance) from Florida State University, she teaches Creative Writing at Clayton State University where she is Associate Professor of English. She is also an editorial reviewer for *Confluence: The Journal of Graduate Liberal Studies*. Brigitte lives in Atlanta.

KEVIN CANTWELL has published two books of poetry, *Something Black in the Green Part of Your Eye* (2002) and *One of Those Russian Novels* (2009). He edited the anthology *Writing on Napkins at the Sunshine Club: An Anthology of Poets Writing in Macon* (2011). He chairs the Department of Media, Culture, and the Arts and Middle Georgia State College.

MARIAN CARCACHE'S short story collection, *The Moon and the Star*, was published by Solomon & George Publishers in 2013. Her work has appeared in *Shenandoah, Chattahoochee Review, Southern Humanities Review, Bronte Society Transactions, Birmingham Arts Journal,* and has been anthologized in *Due South, Belles Lettres, Crossroads: Stories of the Southern Literary Fantastic,* and *Climbing Mt. Cheaha: Emerging Alabama Writers. Under the Arbor*, an opera made from her short story and for which she wrote the libretto, appeared on PBS stations nationwide, was nominated for a regional Emmy, and was a finalist in the New York Festivals. She is recipient of the Alabama State Council on the Arts' 2003-2004 Fellowship Award for fiction. Three of her stories have been nominated for the Pushcart Prize. She grew up in rural Russell County, Alabama and now lives in Auburn.

CATHY CARLISI'S poetry has appeared in *The Atlanta Review, Prairie Schooner, The Mid-American Review, Southern Review, The Greensboro Review,* and *Gargoyle*. Her manuscript, *The Natural Order of Things*, has been a finalist in several contests including the Tampa Review Prize for Poetry, Lost Horse Press Idaho Prize for Poetry, Carolina Wren Press, MMM Press Book Prize, Elixir Press Annual Poetry Award, and The Washington Prize.

RICKS CARSON lives and teaches high school in Atlanta, and is a member of the Side Door Poets group. His poems have appeared in a number of magazines, including *The Chattahoochee Review, The Atlanta Review, The Chariton Review, Zone 3,* and *the Kansas Quarterly*. He received Pushcart nominations in 2003 from *Oysterboy Review* for "In the City of God," and in 2005 from *The Hatchling* for "Scary."

JIMMY CARTER is a prolific and adventurous writer. He has published fiction, poetry, and nonfiction. A former President of the United States and Governor of Georgia, he grew up on a farm near Plains and has lived there nearly all his life. His poem, "A Winter Morning," originally appeared in *Negative Capability XIV,* 1994.

KATIE CHAPLE is the author of *Pretty Little Rooms* (Press 53, August 2011), winner of the 2012 Devil's Kitchen Reading Award in Poetry through Southern Illinois University, Carbondale. She teaches poetry and writing at the University of West Georgia and edits *Terminus Magazine*. Her work has appeared or is forthcoming in such journals as *Antioch Review, Crab Orchard Review, New South, Passages North, Southern Indiana Review, StorySouth, The Rumpus, Washington Square,* and others. She was the recipient of *Southern Humanities Review's* Theodore Christian Hoepfner Award. "Pretty Little Rooms" first appeared in *Crab Orchard Review* and also appears in her first book *Pretty Little Rooms*.

DIYA CHAUDHURI'S poems have appeared in *Hayden's Ferry Review, Redivider, Sycamore Review,* and *Smartish Pace*.

SIMONA CHITESCU is a poet, originally from Romania, now living in Atlanta, Georgia, and working towards a PhD in Creative Writing at Georgia State University, where she is also a teaching fellow. Her poems have appeared in print and online publications including *The Adirondack Review* and *Smartish Pace*. "Story in the Late Style of a City" was the recipient of the 46ers Prize from *The Adirondack Review*. "Secrets" was a finalist in 2013 Beullah Rose Poetry contest.

GEORGE DAVID CLARK teaches creative writing and literature as a Lilly Postdoctoral Fellow at Valparaiso University. *Interview Conducted through the Man-Eater's Throat*, his first book, won the Miller William Poetry Prize and is available from *University of Arkansas Press*. His most recent poems can be found or are forthcoming in new issues of *Alaska Quarterly Review, The Antioch Review, Blackbird, FIELD, The Greensboro Review, The Missouri Review, The Southwest Review,* and *The Yale Review*, as well as online at *Verse Daily* and *Poetry Daily*. He is the editor of *32 Poems* and now lives in Indiana with his wife and their two young children.

JIM CLARK was born in Byrdstown, Tennessee, and educated at Vanderbilt University, the University of North Carolina at Greensboro, and the University of Denver. He is the Elizabeth H. Jordan Professor of Southern Literature and Dean of the School of Humanities at Barton College in Wilson, North Carolina. From 1987-1994 he was an Assistant Professor of English and Director of the Creative Writing Program at the University of Georgia. His books include *Notions: A Jim Clark Miscellany*; two collections of poetry, *Dancing on Canaan's Ruins* and *Handiwork*; and he edited *Fable in the Blood: The Selected Poems of Byron Herbert Reece*. His work has appeared in *The Georgia Review, Prairie Schooner, Southern Poetry Review, Denver Quarterly, Greensboro Review,* and *Asheville Poetry Review*.

DANIEL CONLAN is a writer from Newnan, GA who studied at The University of Georgia. His work has been featured in *Stillpoint Literary Magazine, Newnan Coweta Magazine*, and on *The Camel Saloon*.

DANIEL CORRIE'S poetry has been featured in *The American Scholar, Hudson Review, Image, Kenyon Review, The Nation, New Criterion, Shenandoah, Southern Review,* and *Virginia Quarterly Review*. A villanelle of his received the 2011 first-place Morton Marr Poetry Prize for a formal poem and appeared in *The Southwest Review*. Aralia Press (West Chester University) published a long poem in a fine press chapbook edition. Three of his poems recently were included in *The Southern Poetry Anthology: Georgia*, and a long poem of his was featured in the anthology *The Gulf Stream: Poems of the Gulf Coast*. He occasionally writes essays, such as "What Is Human Time?" which appeared in *The Hudson Review* and an essay on rhyme which recently was reprinted in *The Able Muse Anthology*.

TASHA COTTER'S first full-length collection of poetry, *Some Churches*, was released in 2013 with Gold Wake Press. Her work has appeared in or is forthcoming in *NANO Fiction, Verse Daily,* and *The Rumpus*.

BRUCE COVEY'S sixth book of poetry, *Change Machine*, was published in 2014 by Noemi. He lives in Atlanta, GA, where he publishes and edits *Coconut* magazine and Coconut Books and curates the video reading series *What's New in Poetry* for the web community *Real Pants*. He is Small Press Editor of *Boog City* and has taught at Emory University, Yale University, and the Atlanta College of Art.

CHAD DAVIDSON is the author of *From the Fire Hills* (2014), *The Last Predicta* (2008), and *Consolation Miracle* (2003), all from Southern Illinois UP, as well as co-author with Gregory Fraser of two textbooks: *Writing Poetry: Creative and Critical Approaches* and *Analyze Anything*. His poems have appeared in *AGNI, Boston Review, DoubleTake, The Paris Review, Ploughshares,* and *Virginia Quarterly Review*. He is a professor of literature and creative writing at the University of West Georgia.

TRAVIS WAYNE DENTON lives in Atlanta where he is the Associate Director of Poetry @ TECH as well as a McEver Chair in Poetry at Georgia Tech. He is also founding editor of the literary arts publication *Terminus Magazine*. His poems have appeared in *MEAD: a magazine of literature and libations, The Atlanta Review, The Greensboro Review, Washington Square, Forklift, Rattle, Tygerburning, Birmingham Poetry Review,* and the *Cortland Review*. His second collection of poems, *When Pianos Fall from the Sky*, was published in October 2012 by Marick Press.

MELISSA DICKSON is the author of *Cameo* (2011) and *Sweet Aegis, Medusa Poems* (2013). Her poems have appeared in *Shenandoah, North American Review, Southern Humanities Review, Bitter Southerner, Cumberland River Review, Southern Women's Review, Literary Mama,* and *Gravy* from the Southern Foodways Alliance at the University of Mississippi. She teaches at the University of West Georgia. "Taking the Backroads to the Orthodontist" is scheduled to appear in *Southern Humanities Review*.

MICHAEL DIEBERT is the author of *Life Outside the Set* (Sweatshoppe, 2013) and is poetry editor for *The Chattahoochee Review*. He teaches writing and literature at Georgia Perimeter College. Recent poems have appeared in *Flycatcher, Dead Mule School of Southern Literature, jmww,* and *The Comstock Review*. He is a resident of Decatur, Georgia.

MAUDELLE DRISKELL grew up in rural southern Georgia and lived most of her adult life in Atlanta where she was a founding editor of *The Atlanta Review*. She now lives in Bethlehem, New Hampshire, and is the executive director of The Frost Place. She holds an MFA in poetry from Warren Wilson College and she is the recipient of the Ruth Lilly Fellowship, awarded by *Poetry* magazine and the Modern Language Association. Her work has been published in many literary reviews and anthologies. Her first book is forthcoming from Hobblebush Press in 2014.

BLANCHE FARLEY, Dublin, GA, is a native of nearby Wrightsville and has lived and taught in Atlanta (Fulton Co. Schools) and at Young Harris College. Her poems and stories have appeared in *Confrontation, Negative Capability, Southern Humanities Review,* and also in textbooks and anthologies including *The Signet Book of American Humor, Southern Poetry Anthology,* and *The Bedford Introduction to Literature*. "Mason's Bridge" was published in *Bloodroot Literary Magazine*. "Laughter" was published in *Southern Poetry Review* 48:1, Fall 2010 and also appears in the *Southern Poetry Anthology* (V.5), 2012, from Texas Review Press.

ELIZABETH FIELDS, a Cave Canem fellow, has been published in several print and on line publications, including the *Cave Canem Anthology XII, The Mandala Literary Journal,* and *Pluck! The Journal of Affrilachian Arts & Culture*. She graduated with an MFA in 2009 and currently teaches English at the University of North Georgia. "Wishing On a Star" was first published in the *Cave Canem Anthology XII: Poems 2008-2009*. Willow Books, 2012.

RUPERT FIKE'S collection of poems *Lotus Buffet (Brick Road Poetry Press)* was named Finalist in the 2011 Georgia Author of the Year Awards.

He has been nominated for Pushcart prizes in fiction and poetry with work appearing in *The Southern Review of Poetry, Rosebud, Natural Bridge, The Georgetown Review, A & U America's AIDS Magazine,* and *The Buddhist Poetry Review*. He has a poem inscribed in a downtown Atlanta plaza, and his non-fiction, *Voices from The Farm,* is now in its second printing with accounts of life on a spiritual commune in the 1970s. "Bacon Grease" appeared in the 2013 prize edition of *Alligator Juniper.*

ANN FISHER-WIRTH'S fourth book of poems, *Dream Cabinet,* was published by Wings Press in 2012. Her other books of poems are *Carta Marina, Blue Window,* and *Five Terraces,* and the chapbooks *The Trinket Poems, Walking Wu-Wei's Scroll,* and *Slide Shows.* She coedited *The Ecopoetry Anthology,* published by Trinity University Press early in 2013. Her poems appear widely and have received numerous awards, including a Malahat Review Long Poem Prize, the Rita Dove Poetry Award, the Mississippi Institute of Arts and Letters Poetry Award, two Mississippi Arts Commission fellowships, and thirteen Pushcart nominations including a Special Mention. Ann has had a senior Fulbright lectureship to the University of Fribourg, Switzerland, and has held the Fulbright Distinguished Chair at Uppsala University, Sweden. In 2006 she was President of the Association for the Study of Literature and Environment. She teaches at the University of Mississippi, where she also directs the minor in Environmental Studies. She also teaches yoga at Southern Star Yoga Studio in Oxford, MS.

GREGORY FRASER is a poet, editor, and professor. He is the author of three poetry collections: *Strange Pietà, Answering the Ruins,* and *Designed for Flight.* He is the co-author, with poet Chad Davidson, of two college textbooks, *Writing Poetry* and *Analyze Anything.* Fraser grew up in Philadelphia and its suburbs, and earned a B.A. at Ursinus College, an MFA at Columbia University, and a Ph.D. at the University of Houston. His poetry has appeared in such journals as *The Paris Review, The Southern Review, The Gettysburg Review,* and *Ploughshares.* The recipient of a grant from the National Endowment for the Arts and the 2010 Georgia Author of the Year in Poetry, Fraser teaches at the University of West Georgia, located an hour west of Atlanta, and serves as features editor of the *Birmingham Poetry Review.*

ALICE FRIMAN'S fifth full-length collection is *Vinculum* (LSU) for which she won the 2012 Georgia Author of the Year Award in Poetry. She is a recipient of a 2012 Pushcart Prize and is included in *Best American Poetry 2009.* Her collection *The View from Saturn* is also available from LSU. Friman lives in Milledgeville, Georgia, where she is Poet-in-Residence at

Georgia College. Her podcast series, *Ask Alice,* is sponsored by the Georgia College MFA program and can be seen on YouTube. "Red Camellia" was first published in *The Georgia Review.*

HESTER L. ("LEE") FUREY has taught at the Art Institute of Atlanta for more than 15 years. The author of *Little Fish* (a chapbook of poems published by Finishing Line Press) and the editor of *Dictionary of Literary Biography 345: American Radical and Reform Writers, Second Series,* Furey has published a number of poems and essays in scholarly and literary journals and is a founding editor of the online journal *eyedrum periodically.* She lives in Decatur, Georgia.

ELIZABETH CRANFORD GARCIA'S work has appeared in *Boxcar Poetry Review, 491 Magazine, Irreantum, Poets and Artists, Blue Lake Review,* and *Red River Review,* as well as in a recent anthology, *Fire in the Pasture: 21st Century Mormon Poets.* She has worked as editor for *The Reach of Song,* the anthology for the Georgia Poetry Society, and serves on the *Segullah* poetry board.

SARAH GORDON is the author of the poetry collection *Distances* (Brito & Lair, 1999), *Flannery O'Connor: The Obedient Imagination* (UGA Press 2000), *A Literary Guide to Flannery O'Connor's Georgia* (UGA Press 2008), and editor of *Flannery O'Connor: In Celebration of Genius* (Hill Street P, University South Carolina Press 1999, 2010). Her poems have appeared in journals throughout the country, including *Shenandoah, Georgia Review, Apalachee Quarterly, Frontiers, Calyx, Confrontation, Southern Poetry Review,* and *Descant,* and *Arts & Letters* (forthcoming). She lives in Athens, Georgia. Her poem, "Apertures: Andalusia" first appeared in *Broad River Review* and won First Prize in the BRR's Ron Rash Poetry Contest in 2010.

ROBERT GRAY is the author of three books of poems: *Jesus Walks the Southland* (2014), *DREW: Poems from Blue Water* (2009), and *I Wish That I Were Langston Hughes* (2008), all from Negative Capability Press. He is also the director of *Mobile in Black and White,* an award-winning documentary film project that explores race relations in Mobile, Alabama. He has taught writing and literature at the University of Alabama, Michigan State University, and Troy State University. He currently works in the Innovation in Learning Center at the University of South Alabama, where he also teaches for the English Department. He holds a B.A. and M.A. in English and a Ph.D. in Instructional Technology from the University of Alabama.

BETH GYLYS, a professor at Georgia State University, has published two award-winning collections of poetry, *Spot in the Dark* (Ohio State University Press) and *Bodies that Hum* (Silverfish Review Press), and two chapbooks, *Matchbook* (La Vita Poetica Press) and *Balloon Heart* (Wind Press). Awarded fellowships and residencies at the MacDowell Colony, La Muse and La Centre D'art i Natura de Farrera, her work has been widely published in anthologies and journals including *Paris Review, Antioch Review, Kenyon Review, Ploughshares, Boston Review*, and *The Southern Review*.

D.L. HALL'S writing can be found in the collection *Becoming: What Makes a Woman* (University of Nebraska Press, 2012), *Apalachee Review, The Arkansas Review, River Teeth, The Sun, The Literary Review*, and *International Quarterly*. The 2nd edition of her creative writing textbook *The Anatomy of Narrative: Analyzing Fiction and Creative Nonfiction* came out in 2012 (Kendall/Hunt). She currently teaches creative writing at Valdosta State University in Georgia and lives in Valdosta.

DERRICK HARRIELL was born and raised in Milwaukee, Wisconsin. He's worked as assistant poetry editor for *Third World Press* and *The Cream City Review* and has taught community writing workshops. Harriell's poems have appeared in various literary journals and anthologies. His two poetry collections, *Cotton* (2010) and *Ropes* (2013), are both from Aquarius Press-Willow Books. He is a Professor of English and African-American studies at The University of Mississippi.

PAMELA HART is writer in residence at the Katonah Museum of Art where she manages a visual literacy arts in education program. She was awarded an NEA creative writing fellowship in 2013. She's a mentor for the Afghan Women's Writing Project. Her chapbook *The End of the Body* was published by Toadlily Press. Her poetry has been published in a variety of journals.

WILLIAM OGDEN HAYNES is a poet and author of short fiction from Alabama who was born in Michigan and grew up a military brat. His first book of poetry entitled P*oints of Interest* appeared in 2012 and a second collection of poetry and short stories *Uncommon Pursuits* was published in 2013. Both are available on Amazon in Kindle and paperback. He has also published over eighty poems and short stories in literary journals and anthologies.

M. AYODELE HEATH is the author of *Otherness* (Brick Road Poetry Press) and editor of the anthology, *Electronic Corpse: Poems from a Digital Salon*. Recipient of fellowships to Caversham Centre for Artists (South Africa) and Cave Canem, he is a top individual 10-finisher at the National Poetry Slam. A graduate of the MFA in Poetry at New England College, he is a former McEver Visiting Chair in Writing at Georgia Tech. His work has appeared widely in journals and anthologies including *diode, Muzzle, Crab Orchard Review, Mississippi Review, storySouth,* and India's *International Gallerie.*

GRAHAM HILLARD is an associate professor of English at Trevecca Nazarene University and the editor of *The Cumberland River Review.* He has contributed poetry to T*he Believer, Image, Notre Dame Review,* and numerous other journals and has written for *The Los Angeles Review of Books, The Oxford American, The Weekly Standard,* and other magazines. He has been a resident fellow on several occasions at the Virginia Center for the Creative Arts, a Tennessee Williams Scholar at the Sewanee Writers' Conference, and a finalist for the Livingston Award for Young Journalists.

LAURENCE HOLDEN is a writer and visual artist who lives in the North Georgia Mountains. His poems have appeared in Chrysalis Reader (*Lenses on Reality , Your Turn,* and *It's a Deal: Dynamic Transactions*), as well as in *Appalachian Heritage,* 2011, three issues of *The Reach of Song: The Poetry Anthology of the Georgia Poetry Society,* 2011, 2010, 2013, and *The Written River 2012.* His work received an award of excellence from the Georgia Poetry Society in 2010, an honorable mention from the Byron Herbert Reece Society in 2011 and the Porter Fleming Award in 2011. His paintings have appeared in over 20 solo exhibits, and are in over 200 public, private, and corporate collections.

KAREN PAUL HOLMES'S full-length poetry collection, *Untying the Knot,* is forthcoming from Alabaster Leaves. Her poetry has appeared in publications such as *Atlanta Review, POEM, The Sow's Ear Poetry Review, American Society: What Poets See* (FutureCycle Press), and *The Southern Poetry Anthology Vol 5: Georgia* (Texas Review Press). She splits her time between Atlanta and the North Georgia Mountains.

H. HOLT has been published a handful of times, most recently by *Off With.* She is currently a member of The Southern Collective Experience, a group of individuals striving to strengthen all aspects of Southern artistic expression. She lives in the luscious mountains of North Georgia.

PETER HUGGINS fourth book of poems is *South*; his previous books of poems are *Necessary Acts, Blue Angels,* and *Hard Facts.* Over 300 poems appear in more than 100 journals, magazines, and anthologies, including *Alabama Literary Review, Apalachee Review, The Chattahoochee Review, Colorado Review, Dickinson Review, Louisiana Literature, Mississippi Review, Natural Bridge, North Dakota Quarterly, Solo, Southern Humanities Review,* and *The Texas* Review. He has also published a picture book, *Trosclair and* *the Alligator*, and a middle grade novel, *In the Company of Owls*. *Trosclair* has appeared on the PBS show *Between the Lions*, received a Mom's Choice Award, and was selected as a best book by CCBC *Choices* at the University of Wisconsin-Madison and by Bank Street College of Education. Among his other awards and honors, Peter Huggins has been a Tennessee Williams Scholar at the Sewanee Writers' Conference and has received a Literature Fellowship in Poetry from the Alabama State Council on the Arts. He teaches in the English Department at Auburn University.

SARA HUGHES has lived in Georgia her entire life. She completed a PhD in English from Georgia State University in 2014. Her poems and reviews have been published in *Rattle, Reed, Rosebud, Atlanta Review, Southern Literary Review, Review Americana, The Oklahoma Review, West Trade Review, Red Clay Review,* and *Arts and Letters*, among others. She teaches at Mercer University and lives in McDonough, Georgia.

T.R. HUMMER'S 11th book of poems, *Skandalon*, was published in 2014 by LSU Press. Formerly editor of *The Kenyon Review*, of *The New England Review*, and of *The Georgia Review*, he has received a Guggenheim Fellowship in Poetry, a poetry NEA, the Hanes Prize for Poetry, the Richard Wright Award for Literary Excellence, and two Pushcart Prizes.

JAMIE IREDELL is the author of *I Was a Fat Drunk Catholic School Insomniac, The Book of Freaks,* and *Prose. Poems. a Novel*. His writing has appeared in many magazines, among them *PANK, Gigantic,* and *The Rumpus*. He lives in Atlanta where he teaches creative writing.

ROBERT PERRY IVEY, born in Forsyth, GA, grew up in Macon and is a visiting assistant professor at Gordon State College and was the Visiting McEver Chair of Poetry at the Georgia Institute of Technology (Georgia Tech) from 2012-2013. Ivey has earned a M.A. in English Literature from Georgia State University and a MFA from Sarah Lawrence College in Creative Writing. He is the author of the chapbook *Southbound*, recipient of Academy of American Poetry's John B. Santoianni Award, and his work has appeared in *The Country Mouse, Louisiana Review, Live Oak Review, At-Large Magazine, Terminus Magazine, Java Monkey Speaks: A Poetry Anthology, G.S.U. Review* (now *New South*), *Blue Lyra Review, TYCA Southeast,* and *Lumina*. "To Home" was first published in *Lumina Vol 7,* 2008.

MIKE JAMES has published seven poetry collections. *Elegy in Reverse* (2014, Aldrich Press) and *Past Due Notices: Poems 1991-2011* (2012, Main Street Rag) are his most recent. He also serves as the associate editor of *The Kentucky Review* and is the publisher of Yellow Pepper Press, a small poetry broadside press. After years spent in South Carolina, Missouri, and Pennsylvania he now lives in Douglasville, Georgia with his wife and five children.

GORDON JOHNSTON, a Georgia native, has lived all but one year of his life in the state. Perkolator Press published his chapbook, *Gravity's Light Grip* in 2008, and his poems have appeared in the Georgia volume of *The Anthology of Southern Poetry* (Texas Review Press) and *Southern Poetry Review*. He regularly wood-fires poems onto tiles and clay bottles in the anagama kiln of Roger Jamison in Juliette, Georgia. His poems, stories, and essays have been published in *The Georgia Review, Many Mountains Moving, Third Genre, Atlanta Review, Denver Quarterly*, and other publications. His conversation with Pattiann Rogers was published in the Spring 2007 *Georgia Review*. He teaches creative writing and contemporary literature at Mercer University in Macon, GA.

MELANIE JORDAN is the author of *Hallelujah for the Ghosties* from Sundress Press (2015) and the chapbook *Ghost Season*. Before receiving her MFA at Southern Illinois Carbondale and her doctorate at University of Houston, she studied at UTC. She teaches at the University of West Georgia. Her work has appeared in *Iowa Review, Birmingham Poetry Review, Third Coast, Southeast Review, Diagram,* and *Black Warrior Review.*

ANDREA JURJEVIĆ is a native of Croatia. Her poems have appeared in *The Journal, Harpur Palate, Raleigh Review, Best New Poets, The Missouri Review*, and elsewhere; her translations can be found in *Lunch Ticket, RHINO,* and *The Adirondack Review*. She is the winner of the 2013 Robinson Jeffers Tor Prize and the 2014 Der-Hovanessian Translation Award. Her translation of "Devil & Freedom" by Olja Savičević Ivančević won the 2015 Rhino translation award.

LISSA KIERNAN'S first book *Two Faint Lines in the Violet* was published by Negative Capability Press. Kiernan holds an MFA from the Stonecoast program at the University of Southern Maine and an MA in Media Studies from The New School for Social Research. She is the founding director of The Rooster Moans Poetry Cooperative.
Two Faint Lines in the Violet was a finalist for Foreword Reviews' 2014 INDIEFAB Book of the Year Awards and also a finalist for the 2014 Julie Suk Award for Best Poetry Book published by an independent press.

ANNA KING is working on a PhD in poetry at Georgia State University in Atlanta, Georgia. Her most recent publications have been featured in *So to Speak, The Unrorean, Antithesis, Stone Highway Review,* and *West Trade* literary magazines, as well as in the *Ellen Glasgow Journal of Southern Women Writers, Florida English,* and *The Apalachee Review.*

BILL KING lived in Athens, GA from 1983-1996. He attended the University of Georgia, receiving an M.A. in Creative Writing (1990), and a Ph.D. in Literature (1995). He now teaches Creative Writing and American Literature at Davis & Elkins College in Elkins, WV, where he directs the D&E Writers' Series. His work has appeared in *The Southern Poetry Anthology, Wild Sweet Notes II: More West Virginia Poetry, XCP: Cross-Cultural Poetics, Nantahala: A Review of Writing and Photography in Appalachia, Still: The Journal,* and *Flycatcher.*

ROBERT S. KING, a native Georgian, now lives in Lexington, Kentucky. His poems have appeared in hundreds of magazines, including *California Quarterly, Chariton Review, Hollins Critic, Kenyon Review, Lullwater Review, Main Street Rag, Midwest Quarterly, Negative Capability, Southern Poetry Review,* and *Spoon River Poetry Review.* He has published four chapbooks (*When Stars Fall Down as Snow*, Garland Press 1976; *Dream of the Electric Eel*, Wolfsong Publications 1982; *The Traveller's Tale*, Whistle Press 1998; and *Diary of the Last Person on Earth*, Sybaritic Press, 2014). His full-length collections are *The Hunted River* and *The Gravedigger's Roots*, both in 2nd editions from FutureCycle Press, 2012; *One Man's Profit* from Sweatshoppe Publications, 2013; and *Developing a Photograph of God* from Glass Lyre Press, 2014.

DOROTHY KNIGHT earned an MFA from University of Mississippi before moving to Chicago last year. Her work has appeared in *Salt Magazine* and *Squaw Valley Review.* She is from Kingsland, GA.

CHRISSY KOLAYA is a poet and fiction writer, author of *Any Anxious Body: poems* (Broadstone Books) and *Charmed Particles: a novel* (Dzanc Books).

KEETJE KUIPERS has been the Margery Davis Boyden Wilderness Writing Resident, a Wallace Stegner Fellow at Stanford University, and the Emerging Writer Lecturer at Gettysburg College. Her first book, *Beautiful in the Mouth*, won the A. Poulin, Jr. Prize from BOA Editions and was published in 2010. Her second book, *The Keys to the Jail,* was published by BOA Editions in 2014. She is an Assistant Professor at Auburn University. "Georgia" was originally published in *Cheat River Review.*

IRENE LATHAM was born in Covington, Georgia, and has made her home in Birmingham, Alabama since 1984. She serves as poetry editor for *Birmingham Arts Journal.* The author of three collections of poems for adults, she has also written two award-winning novels for children, *Leaving Gee's Bend* and *Don't Feed the Boy*. Her first book of poems for children *Dear Wandering Wildebeest* is available from Millbrook Press/Lerner.

JOSHUA LAVENDER writes poems that explore landscape and the moment's ephemerality. His work has appeared in *Free State Review, Able Muse, Town Creek Poetry,* and *The Southern Poetry Anthology*. A graduate of Georgia College & State University and the MFA poetry program at the University of Maryland, College Park, Joshua is presently working with Plamen Press in Washington, D.C., on a co-translation of the Czech poet Vitezslav Nezval's collection *Farewell and a Handkerchief*.

HANK LAZER has published seventeen books of poetry, including *Portions* (Lavender Ink, 2009), *The New Spirit* (Singing Horse, 2005), *Elegies & Vacations* (Salt, 2004), and *Days* (Lavender Ink, 2002). Lazer's seventeenth book of poetry *N18 (complete)*, a handwritten book, is available from Singing Horse Press. In 2011, in collaboration with visual artists from the Taller Experimental de Gráfica in Havana and the University of Alabama's Book Arts program, Lazer published *Indivisible*, a fine press bilingual edition of handwritten shape poems. Pages from the notebooks have been performed with soprano saxophonist Andrew Raffo Dewar, including performances at the University of Georgia and in Havana, Cuba. Over the past fifteen years, Lazer has collaborated with various jazz musicians, filmmakers, choreographers, and visual artists in seeking new ways to present poetry. In 2008, *Lyric & Spirit: Selected Essays, 1996-2008* was published by Omnidawn. With co-editor Charles Bernstein, Lazer edits the Modern and Contemporary Poetics Series for the University of Alabama Press. He is the recipient of the 2015 Harper Lee Award from the Alabama Writer's Forum.

RACHEL VAN HORN LEROY was born in South Georgia and attended Georgia Southern University, where she received her B.A. and M.A. in English Literature. She obtained her MFA in Creative Writing at Sewanee School of Letters at University of the South. She has been an instructor of writing and composition in the Department of Writing and Linguistics at Georgia Southern University since 2002. Rachel publishes in various genres.

KATHLEEN BREWIN LEWIS is a Georgia writer who currently lives in Atlanta, but was born and raised in Savannah. Her poetry and prose have appeared or are forthcoming in *Yemassee, James Dickey Review, STILL: The Journal, Southern Humanities Review, Foundling Review, Heron Tree, The Southern Women's Review,* and *The Southern Poetry Anthology*

Vol. V: Georgia. A graduate of Wake Forest University, she has an MA in Professional Writing from Kennesaw State University. She's been nominated for a Pushcart Prize and is senior editor of *Flycatcher.* "Eggshell" was published online in *Foundling Review.*

JOHN LOWTHER'S work appears in *An Atlanta Poets Group Anthology: The Lattice Inside* (UNO Press, 2012) and *Another South: Experimental Writing in the South* (University of Alabama, 2003). *Held to the Letter,* co-authored with Dana Lisa Young is forthcoming from Lavender Ink in 2015. He is the author of a number of chapbooks, limited editions, and including *Reading Two* (811 Books), *Aeros in Err* (Seeing Eye Books), *.1 [point one]* (Poets and Poets Press) and *Jack Spicer, Poet* (THE NAMELESS). He edits the small press 3rdness, and previously the magazines *SYNTACTICS* and *108*. From 1997 until 2012 he was one of the central figures in the Atlanta Poets Group and between 2003 and 2010 he curated forty-five Language Harm shows (poetry), as well as the smaller series Word & Praxis (critical responses to poets and artists) and Art Performs (performance art) and an international visual poetry show "Unreadability," all at Eyedrum Art and Music Gallery. His first Johnny Minotaur episode was given in 2001 and he tended to give between 6 and 8 of these each year (ranging between 20 minutes and an hour each) before the "final episode" was delivered in the summer of 2009. Many of these improvisations were collaborations with local musicians. A full episode, dating from 2004, is included in *The Lattice Inside.* John also works in video, photography, paint, performance, assemblage and other mediums. He's writing a dissertation in which he reimagines psychoanalysis to include intersex and transgender lives as foundational for understanding subjective possibility.

THOMAS LUX was born in Massachusetts in December 1946 and graduated from Emerson College. He has been awarded grants and fellowships from the Guggenheim Foundation and the Mellon Foundation. He is a three-time recipient of NEA grants. In 1994, he was awarded the Kinglsey Tufts Prize for his book *Split Horizon.* The most recent of his 12 full-length poetry collections is *Child Made of Sand* (Houghton Mifflin Harcourt, 2012). He also recently published *From the Southland* (Marick Press, 2012, nonfiction). BloodAxe Books published his *Selected Books* in the UK in 2014. A book of poems, *Zehntausend Herrliche Jahre,* in German, trs. Klaus Martens, was published in early 2011. Currently, he is Bourne Professor of Poetry and Director of the McEver Visiting Writers program at the Georgia Institute of Technology, as well as Director of Poetry@Tech.

CLARENCE MAJOR began teaching at UC Davis after holding positions at Temple University, SUNY – Binghamton, University of

Colorado, University of Washington, Howard University, Sarah Lawrence College, and Brooklyn College. He writes poetry and fiction as well as non-fiction. He was recently nominated for the 1999 National Book Award in poetry for *Configurations: New & Selected Poems* 1958-1998 (Copper Canyon Press, 1999). His other recent books include *Necessary Distance: Essays and Criticism* (1998), and *All-Night Visitors* (1998). Major reviews for *The Washington Post Book World* and has contributed to *The New York Times, The New York Times Book Review, The Los Angeles Times Book World, American Vision, Essence, Ploughshares, The Kenyon Review, The American Review, The Review of Contemporary Fiction,* and *The American Poetry Review.* In 1991 he served as fiction judge for The National Book Awards. He has served twice on National Endowment for the Arts panels, and in 1997-98 he served as judge for the Pen/Faulkner Awards. He has traveled extensively and lived in various parts of the United States and for extended periods in France and Italy. Clarence Major currently lives in northern California.

CHRISTOPHER MARTIN authored the poetry chapbooks *Everything Turns Away* (La Vita Poetica Press, 2014) and *A Conference of Birds* (New Native Press, 2012). His work has appeared in *The Southern Poetry Anthology, Volume V: Georgia* (Texas Review Press, 2012), *Shambhala Sun, The Good Men Project, Waccamaw, Ruminate Magazine, Thrush Poetry Journal, Still: The Journal, Buddhist Poetry Review, Grit Po: Rough South Poetry* (University of South Carolina Press, 2014), *Town Creek Poetry* and *Pilgrimage*. The editor of *Flycatcher* and a contributing editor at *New Southerner*, Chris lives with his wife and their two young children in northwest Georgia. His full-length poetry collection *Second Coming on South Cobb Drive* (as yet unpublished) has rated highly in national and statewide contests, most recently earning semifinalist in the 2013 Crab Orchard Review Series Open Competition. "Marcescence" was originally published as a broadside by Thrush Press.

KOMAL PATEL MATHEW'S work has appeared in *The New Republic, The Southern Review, The Atlanta Review,* and *The Comstock Review*. Her poetry collection, *Dressing for Diwali,* has also been a finalist for the National Poetry Series Open Competition and a semifinalist for the Alice James Books' Beatrice Hawley Award. She is a Lecturer of English at Kennesaw State University and co-founding editor of *Josephine Quarterly*.

ALAN MAY'S poems have appeared in *New Orleans Review, Double Room: a Journal of Prose Poetry and Flash Fiction, Perihelion, string of small machines, Spell, Willow Springs, The Nervous Breakdown,* and *Phoebe*. He is author of two books: *Dead Letters* (2008) and *More Unknowns* (2014.)

MARIANA MCDONALD'S work has appeared in many publications, including poetry in the *Anthology of Southern Poets: Georgia, Southern Women's Review, Sugar Mule, Fables of the Eco-future; From a Bend in the River: 100 New Orleans Poets,* and *El Boletín Nacional,* and fiction in *UpDo: Flash Fiction by Women Writers* and *So to Speak..* She became a Fellow of Georgia's Hambidge Arts Center in 2012.

PATRICK MCGINN has taught writing and literature at University of Georgia and Columbus State University. He currently teaches at the University of Mississippi.

JESSICA MELILLI-HAND is published in *Barrow Street, The Cortland Review,* and *The Minnesota Review,* among others. She received her BAs in Creative Writing and in Psychology from Carnegie Mellon University and her MFA from Georgia State University, where she is currently pursuing her PhD. She won first place in the Agnes Scott Poetry Competition in 2014, judged by Terrance Hayes, in 2011, judged by Arda Collins, and in 2008, judged by Martín Espada.

JOSEPH VICTOR MILFORD is a Georgia poet who lives south of Atlanta. His first book, *Cracked Altimeter,* was published by BlazeVox press in 2010. He has another book of poems forthcoming from Hydeout Press. He teaches literature courses for eCore and The University of West Georgia. He is also the occasional host of the Joe Milford Poetry Show which has an archive of over 300 interviews with American and Canadian poets.

MICHAEL MILLER is the co-founder of Moon Tide Press and the organizer of the poetry series at the Muckenthaler Cultural Center in Fullerton, California. He is the author of *College Town* (Tebot Bach, 2010) and *The First Thing Mastered* (Tebot Bach, 2013) and has served as a judge for the San Diego Book Awards and Poetry Out Loud.

JUDSON MITCHAM'S work has been widely published in literary journals, including *Poetry, Harper's, Georgia Review, Hudson Review,* and *Southern Review.* His most recent book is *A Little Salvation: Poems Old and New.* He is the current poet laureate of Georgia. In 2013 he was inducted into the Georgia Writers' Hall of Fame.

MAREN O. MITCHELL'S poems have appeared in *Hotel Amerika, Southern Humanities Review, The Classical Outlook, Appalachian Journal, The Arts Journal, Town Creek Poetry Review, Wild Goose Poetry Review, Pirene's Fountain,* anthologies *The Southern Poetry Anthology, V: Georgia, Sunrise from Blue Thunder,* and elsewhere. Work is forthcoming in *The South Carolina Review*. She won 1st Place Award for Excellence in Poetry from the Georgia Poetry Society in 2012. Her nonfiction book is *Beat Chronic Pain, An Insider's Guide* (Line of Sight Press, 2012). "Learning How to Kill" was first published in *Wild Goose Poetry Review*, Fall 2010

SALLY STEWART MOHNEY was awarded the Jesse Rehder Writing Prize from the University of North Carolina at Chapel Hill. Main Street Rag published her poetry chapbook, *pale blue mercy*, as part of their Author's Choice Series. Women Centered Art exhibited her poem installation and Sensoria Arts Festival has staged several of her poems in their productions. She has presented her work at the Southern Women Writers Conferences and has published short stories and poems in many journals. Recently, her poem, "McDowell County Understory," was a finalist in the Ron Rash Poetry Competition. Finishing Line Press just released her chapbook, *A Piece of Calm*. She is the assistant editor of the Georgia Poetry Society's annual anthology, *The Reach of Song*.

JANICE TOWNLEY MOORE, a native of Atlanta, has had a long career teaching English at Young Harris College in the north Georgia mountains. The above poems were published in *Georgia Review*, *Chattahoochee Review*, and *Appalachian Heritage*, respectively and in her chapbook *Teaching the Robins* (Finishing Line Press).

TONY MORRIS is the author of *Pulling at a Thread* (Main Street Rag, upcoming 2015). Other books include: *Back to Cain* (The Olive Press, 2006), and two chapbooks, *Greatest Hits* (Puddinghouse Press, 2012), and *Fugue's End* (Birch Brook Press, 2004). His work has been published in: *Spoon River Review, Hawai'i Review, River Styx, Meridian, The Sewanee Theological Review, South Dakota Review, Connecticut Review, Mississippi Review, Green Mountains Review*, and others. He is the managing editor of *Southern Poetry Review*, and director of the Ossabaw Island Writers' Retreat.

ERIC NELSON has published five poetry collections, including *The Twins* (2009), winner of the Split Oak Press Chapbook Award; *Terrestrials* (2004, Texas Review Press), winner of the X.J. Kennedy Poetry Award; and *The Interpretation of Waking Life* (1991, U. of Arkansas Press), winner of the Arkansas Poetry Award. His poems have appeared in *Poetry, The Southern Review, The Oxford American,* and *The Sun*. He lives in Georgia and teaches at Georgia Southern University.

JEFF NEWBERRY is the author of *Brackish* (Aldrich Press) and the chapbook *A Visible Sign* (Finishing Line Press). With Brent House, he is the co-editor of the anthology *The Gulf Stream: Poems of the Gulf Coast* (Snake

Nation Press). The Poet in Residence at Abraham Baldwin Agricultural College in Tifton, Georgia, he has published work most recently in *Birmingham Poetry Review, Bayou,* and *Chattahoochee Review.*

LAURAH NORTON teaches at Georgia State University, where she earned her MFA in 2006. Her work has appeared in a variety of journals and magazines, including *The Berkeley Review, Post Road, Night Train, Fringe,* and *Failbette*r. Twice, she placed first in *Creative Loafing's* annual fiction contest.

NICK NORWOOD'S poems have appeared in a wide range of journals including *The Paris Review, Shenandoah, Southwestern American Literature, The Wallace Stevens Journal,* and *Poetry Daily*. His third full volume of poetry, *Gravel and Hawk*, won the Hollis Summers Prize in Poetry and was published by Ohio University Press in 2012. His other books are *A Palace for the Heart* (2004) and *The Soft Blare* (2003), and the limited edition, fine press book *Wrestle* (2007), produced in collaboration with the artist Erika Adams. He teaches at Columbus State University in Georgia.

CHRISTINA OLSON is the author of *Before I Came Home Naked*, a book of poems. Her poetry and nonfiction has appeared in magazines and journals including *The Southern Review, Brevity, River Styx, Gulf Coast, Passages North, The Normal School, Hayden's Ferry Review,* and *The Best Creative Nonfiction, Volume 3*. She is the poetry editor of Midwestern Gothic and teaches writing at Georgia Southern University.

LEE PASSARELLA acts as senior literary editor for *Atlanta Review* magazine and served as editor-in-chief of Coreopsis Books, a poetry-book publisher. He also writes classical music reviews for *Audiophile Audition*. Passarella's poetry has appeared in *Chelsea, Cream City Review, Louisville Review, The Formalist, Antietam Review, Journal of the American Medical Association, The Literary Review, Edge City Review, The Wallace Stevens Journal, Snake Nation Review, Umbrella, Slant,* and *Cortland Review*. *Swallowed up in Victory*, Passarella's long narrative poem based on the American Civil War, was published by White Mane Books in 2002. Poet Andrew Hudgins described it as a work "compelling and engrossing as a novel." Passarella has published two poetry collections: *The Geometry of Loneliness* (David Robert Books, 2006) and *Redemption* (FutureCycle Press, 2014). His poetry chapbook *Sight-Reading Schumann* was published by Pudding House Publications in 2007.

LYNN PEDERSEN'S poems, essays, and reviews have appeared in *New England Review, The Comstock Review, Poet Lore, The Southern Poetry*

Review, The Palo Alto Review, Ecotone, and *Heron Tree.* Her chapbook, *Theories of Rain,* was published by Main Street Rag in 2009. A graduate of the Vermont College of Fine Arts, she lives in Atlanta, Georgia.

OLIVER TIMKEN PERRIN is an author and editor, whose published academic work explores the history of human mark use, as well as our contemporary use of marks such as commercial brand insignia. He arrived in Atlanta, Georgia in 1979; with the exception of a whirlwind year and a half spent living in San Francisco, and six years in Istanbul, Georgia has since remained his home. He has been writing poetry for the last 20 years. His early work appears in the online literary underground review *Bohemian Ink.*

PATRICK PHILLIPS'S third book of poems, *Elegy for a Broken Machine,* is forthcoming from Alfred A. Knopf in 2015. He is also the author of *Boy* and *Chattahoochee,* which won the 2005 Kate Tufts Discovery Award. A former Guggenheim and NEA Fellow, his recent honors include the Lyric Poetry Award from the Poetry Society of America, the Emily Clark Balch Prize from *Virginia Quarterly Review,* and a Puschcart Prize. He lives in Brooklyn and teaches at Drew University.

STEPHEN ROGER POWERS started writing poetry thirteen years ago to pass time in the middle of the night when he was too energized to sleep after coming off the stage in comedy clubs around the Midwest. He is the author of *Hello, Stephen* and *The Follower's Tale,* both published by Salmon Poetry. He hasn't done stand-up in a long time, but every once in a while he finds avenues for the performer he was born to be.

RANDY PRUNTY lives in Colorado.

WYATT PRUNTY, director of the Sewanee Writers' Conference, is the Carlton Professor of English at Sewanee and the author of eight collections of poetry. His first, *Domestic of the Outer Banks,* appeared in 1980. *The Times Between* (1982), *What Women Know, What Men Believe* (1986), *Balance as Belief* (1989), *The Run of the House* (1993), *Since the Noon Mail Stopped* (1997), *Unarmed and Dangerous* (2000), and *The Lover's Guide to Trapping* (2009) have subsequently been published by The Johns Hopkins University Press. His critical work, *"Fallen from the Symboled World": Precedents for the New Formalism,* is available from Oxford University Press. In 2005, he was elected to the Fellowship of Southern Writers, where he now serves as Vice-Chancellor. Other honors include Guggenheim, Rockefeller, Johns Hopkins, and Brown Foundation fellowships. Editor of Sewanee Writers on Writing (Louisiana State University Press, 2000), he serves as general editor of the Sewanee Writers' Series and directs the Tennessee Williams Fellowship program at Sewanee.

JANISSE RAY is a writer, naturalist, and activist. She is the author of five books of literary nonfiction, including the acclaimed *Ecology of a Cracker Childhood*, and a collection of nature poetry. Her most recent book is *The Seed Underground: A Growing Revolution to Save Food*, a look at what's happening to seeds, which is to say the future of food. Ray is the William Kittredge Distinguished Visiting Writer at the University of Montana 2014. She holds an MFA from the University of Montana and in 2007 was awarded an honorary doctorate from Unity College in Maine. She lives on an organic farm in southern Georgia.

ANDREA ROGERS was born and bred in south Georgia. Rogers currently resides in Atlanta, where she is a musician and a Ph.D. Poetry student at Georgia State University. Her poetry and creative nonfiction appear in *Mother is a Verb* (Red Paint Hill), *Treehouse*, *Odradek*, and *The 11th Hour*. She and her band, Night Driving in Small Towns, have appeared in features by *Rolling Stone* and NPR.

ROSEMARY ROYSTON, author of *Splitting the Soil* (Finishing Line Press, 2014), resides in northeast Georgia, where she was born and raised. Rosemary's poetry has been published in journals such as *Southern Poetry Review, NANO Fiction, The Comstock Review, Main Street Rag, Coal Hill Review, Flycatcher, STILL, Town Creek Review,* and *Alehouse*.

JAMES SANDERS is a member of the Atlanta Poets Group, a writing and performing collective. His most recent book is *Goodbye Public and Private* (BlazeVox). His book, *Self-Portrait in Plants*, is forthcoming in 2015 from Coconut Books. The University of New Orleans Press also recently published the group's *An Atlanta Poets Group Anthology: The Lattice Inside*.

MIKE SAYE is an MFA student at Georgia State University where he teaches and works as an editorial assistant at *Five Points: A Journal of Literature and Art*. He was born in Canton, Georgia. His work was published in *Rattle's* Tribute to Southern Poets issue. You can follow him on Twitter at Mike_Saye23.

EMILY SCHULTEN is a poet from Bowling Green, Kentucky. She is the author of *Rest in Black Haw* from New Plains Press. Her poems appear widely in nationally recognized journals such as *Prairie Schooner, New Ohio Review, New Orleans Review, Fifth Wednesday, Mid-American Review, North American Review, Salamander, The Los Angeles Review,* and others.

RON SELF is an attorney/musician and teaches in the Turner College of Business at Columbus State University. His work has appeared in *Atlanta Review, Cortland Review, Main Street Rag, The English Review, Birmingham Arts Journal* and various local and area anthologies. He regularly hosts poetry open mic events and is a founding editor of Brick Road Poetry Press.

NANCY SIMPSON, born in Miami, Florida to Georgians, lived her first five years in Atlanta. As an adult she lived in Macon and Dalton and now lives across the Georgia line on a mountain in western North Carolina. She is the author of three poetry collections*: Across Water, Night Student* and most recently *Living Above the Frost Line, New and Selected Poems* (Carolina Wren Press, 2010). She edited *Echoes Across the Blue Ridge* (anthology 2010). She holds an MFA from Warren Wilson College and a BS in Education from Western Carolina University. She cofounded NC Writers Network West, a nonprofit, professional writing organization serving writers from the mountains west of Asheville and the Georgia Mountains. Simpson's poems have been published in *The Georgia Review, Southern Poetry Review, Seneca Review, New Virginia Review,* and *Prairie Schooner.*

JAMES MALONE SMITH from Savannah, Georgia was the editor of *Don't Leave Hungry: Fifty Years of Southern Poetry Review* (University of Arkansas Press, 2009). Co-Editor: *Southern Poetry Review*. His poems have appeared in *Agni, Prairie Schooner, Quarterly West, Shenandoah,* and *32 Poems.* "Smartmouth at Large" and "Smartmouth and The Mysteries" were originally published in *32 Poems*, 11:1, Spring/Summer 2013

R.T. (ROD) SMITH was born in Washington, DC, and grew up in Georgia and North Carolina. He earned a BA in philosophy from the University of North Carolina-Charlotte and an MA in English from Appalachian State University. His collections of poetry include *From the High Dive* (1983), *The Cardinal Heart* (1991), *Hunter-Gatherer* (1996), *Trespasser: Poems* (1996), *Split the Lark: Selected Poems* (1999), *Messenger* (2001), *Brightwood* (2003), *The Hollow Log Lounge* (2003), *Outlaw Style: Poems* (2008), and *In the Night Orchard, Selected Poems* (2015). He has received grants from the National Endowment for the Arts and the Virginia Commission for the Arts and has won the Cohen Prize from *Ploughshares* and three Pushcart Prizes. Smith taught at Auburn University, where he was coeditor of *Southern Humanities Review.* He is writer-in-residence at Washington and Lee University in Lexington, Virginia, where he has served as the editor of *Shenandoah* since 1995. A four-time finalist, Smith has twice received the Library of Virginia Book of the Year Award. He has also been the guest writer-in-residence at VMI and Converse and will, in the fall, be Rachel Rivers-Coffee Distinguished Professor of Creative Writing at Appalachian State.

GREGORY VINCENT ST. THOMASINO has a degree in philosophy from Fordham University. In 2009 he received the Distinguished Scholar Award from the Doctor of Arts in Leadership program at Franklin Pierce University in New Hampshire. His works include *The Logoclasody Manifesto* (Eratio Editions, 2008) and a new book of poems entitled, *The Valise* (Dead Academics, 2012). In his spare time he writes at his blog, The Postmodern Romantic, and edits the online poetry journal, Eratio. "Mercury" and "Anselm" were written in the Atlanta airport.

JOHN STEPHENS is a poet, memoirist, and businessman, living in Milton, Georgia. He is an outspoken community activist and staunch supporter of madd (Mothers Against Drunk Driving). His gifts have helped to establish the Adam Stephens Night Out for Poetry at the Georgia Institute of Technology's Poetry @ TECH series.

TODD STILES was raised in south Arkansas and received his BA in English from the University of Arkansas at Monticello in 1990. He moved to Athens, Georgia in 1994, where he met and married the woman of his dreams, an English PhD from the University of Georgia. They're currently raising their two kids, ages 10 & 3, and still managing to learn something new and vital every single day.

DR. LEON STOKESBURY is the Architect of the Georgia State University's studio/academic Master of Fine Arts degree in creative writing, established in 1989. He also teaches undergraduate and graduate courses in poetry writing, the form and theory of poetry, modern poetry, and contemporary poetry. His poems have appeared in many journals, including *The Partisan Review*, *The Kenyon Review*, *The New Yorker*, *The Georgia Review*, and *The New England Review*, and they have been reprinted in more than three dozen anthologies and college textbooks. His first book of poems, *Often in Different Landscapes*, was chosen by Richard Eberhart as co-winner of the first Associated Writing Programs Poetry Competition (1975). His most recent book of poems is *Autumn Rhythm: New and Selected Poems*, published in 1996. Recently, he edited a second edition of *The Made Thing: An Anthology of Contemporary Southern Poetry*, published in 2000. Dr. Stokesbury has received numerous grants and awards for his poetry, including the Porter Fund Award for Literary Excellence (1985), the Robert Frost Fellowship in Poetry from the Breadloaf Writers Conference (1990), and the Distinguished Georgia Poet of the Year Award (1992). Autumn Rhythm: New and Selected Poems was awarded The Poet's Prize for 1996 as the best book of verse published by an American citizen during that year.

RUSSELL STREUR is a resident of Johns Creek, Georgia. His poetry has been published widely internationally and within the United States.

He operates the world's original on-line poetry bar, *The Camel Saloon*, is the author of *The Muse of Many Names* (Poets Democracy, 2011) and *Table of Discontents* (Ten Pages Press, 2012), and has twice has won awards for excellence from the Georgia Poetry Society (2012, 2013). His collection *Faultlines* is forthcoming from New Plains Press.

CHRISTINE SWINT holds an MFA in creative writing/poetry from Georgia State University. She received an MA in Spanish language and literature from Middlebury College and has worked as an instructor of both English and Spanish. She has taught courses in poetry writing and composition, and she has trained with Amherst Writers and Artists to lead creative writing workshops. The AWA method encourages creative expression and respects the writer's original voice. Her poems appear in *Slant, a Journal of Poetry, Tampa Review, Southern Women's Review, Broad River Review* (Spring 2014), *Birmingham Poetry Review* (Spring 2015), and others. Her poems have been nominated for the Pushcart Prize, Best of the Net, and Best New Poets. She lives in metro Atlanta, Georgia with her husband, their two sons, and her dogs, Red and Duffy.

MARIANNE SZLYK is an associate professor of English at Montgomery College, an associate poetry editor at Potomac Review, and the editor of T*he Song Is…*, a site for poems inspired by music. Her own poems have appeared in print and online, most recently in *The Camel Saloon, Poppy Road Review, Jellyfish Whispers, Poetry Pacific, The Blue Hour Literary Magazine,* and *Storm Cycle 2013: The Best of Kind of a Hurricane Press*. Other publications, including her first chapbook, are forthcoming.

ALICE TEETER served as an Adjunct Professor, Lecturer in Poetry, at Emory University in Atlanta, Georgia, from 2011 through 2013. She studied poetry at Eckerd College with Peter Meinke. Her chapbook entitled *20 CLASS A* was published in 1975 by Morningstar Media, Tallahassee, Florida. Her collection of poems entitled String Theory won the Georgia Poetry Society's 2008 Charles B. Dickson Chapbook Contest, judged by poet Lewis Turco and her book *When It Happens To You . . .* was published in 2009 by Star Cloud Press. Teeter co-leads 'Improvoetry' workshops with actor/director/creative coach Lesly Fredman, using improvisation techniques as poetic inspiration and poetry as a springboard for further improvisation. She is a member of Alternate ROOTS, a service organization for artists doing community-based work in the Southeast and is also a member of the Artist Conference Network, a national coaching community for people doing creative work. With her partner, Kathie deNobriga, she hosts a monthly Art Salon where artists of all kinds present finished work or work in progress to small, but appreciative audiences. "This Quiet Lake" was published online in *The Tower Journal,* Fall 2012,Volume 5, Number 1.

JESSICA TEMPLE earned her BA from the University of Alabama and her MA from Mississippi State University. She is currently a PhD student in poetry at Georgia State University, where she works for the syndicated poetry college radio show *Melodically Challenged* and reads for Five Points. Her work has recently appeared in *Loose Change Magazine, Red Clay Review, Birmingham Arts Journal,* and *decomP magazinE*. Her chapbook, *Seamless and Other Legends*, is available from Finishing Line Press.

PATRICIA PERCIVAL THOMAS lives in Atlanta, Georgia, where she thinks about the big picture while micromanaging her garden (weeding). Five of her poems can be found in *Sixfold*. Her poems also appear in *The Southern Poetry Anthology, Volume 5: Georgia; Town Creek Poetry; Stonepile Writer's Anthology, Volume II* and other venues. Her chapbook, *Bargain with the Speed of Light*, is available from Kattywompus Press in 2014.

JEANIE THOMPSON recent collection is *The Myth of Water: From the Life of Helen Keller*. Her poems have recently appeared in *Kenyon Review Online, The Southern Women's Review, PoemMemoirStory, The New Sound,* and *Thirty-Three*, an anthology of Negative Capability Press. "Coming through Fire" was a finalist in the 2014 Richard Peterson Poetry Prize and is forthcoming in *The Crab Orchard Review*. Jeanie's previous poetry collections include *The Seasons Bear Us, White for Harvest, Witness,* and *How to Enter the River*. She teaches in the Spalding University low residency MFA Writing Program (Louisville KY) and is founding executive director of the Alabama Writers' Forum (Montgomery).

NATASHA TRETHEWEY earned an MA in poetry from Hollins University and an MFA in poetry from the University of Massachusetts. Her first collection of poetry, *Domestic Work* (Graywolf Press, 2000), was selected by Rita Dove as the winner of the inaugural Cave Canem Poetry Prize for the best first book by an African American poet and won both the 2001 Mississippi Institute of Arts and Letters Book Prize and the 2001 Lillian Smith Award for Poetry. Since then, she has published three more collections of poetry, including *Thrall* (Houghton Mifflin, 2012); *Native Guard* (Houghton Mifflin, 2006), which received the Pulitzer Prize for Poetry; and *Bellocq's Ophelia* (Graywolf Press, 2002). In 2012, Trethewey was named as both the state poet laureate of Mississippi and the 19th U.S. poet laureate by the Library of Congress. In 2013, she was appointed for a second term.

MEMYE CURTIS TUCKER, born in Atlanta, is the author of *The Watchers* (Hollis Summers Poetry Prize, Ohio University Press), which in

2010 was named by the Georgia Center for the Book one of three poetry "Books All Georgians Should Read," and author of three prizewinning chapbooks; poems in *Poetry Daily, the Georgia, Colorado, Southern,* and *Southern Poetry Reviews, Negative Capability, Prairie Schooner, Shenandoah,* and other journals and anthologies. Recipient of a PhD in English and fellowships from the Georgia Council for the Arts, MacDowell, and VCCA, she teaches advanced poetry writing and is a Senior Editor of Atlanta Review.

DAN VEACH is the founder and editor of Atlanta Review and author of Elephant Water, winner of the Georgia Author of the Year Award in poetry. A translator of Chinese, Arabic, and Anglo-Saxon, Dan has won the Willis Barnstone Translation Prize. He is editor and co-translator of *Flowers of Flame: Unheard Voices of Iraq* (Michigan State University Press, 2008), which won an Independent Publisher Book Award. In 2008 he was honored with the Lifetime Achievement Award from the Georgia Writers Association. Dan has performed his poetry worldwide, including Oxford University, People's University in Beijing, the American University in Cairo, and the Adelaide Festival in Australia. He is also a clarinetist and composer whose work has been performed by bands and orchestras.

SHARON VENEZIO is the author of *The Silence of Doorways* (March 2013, Moon Tide Press). Her poems have appeared in *Spillway, Bellevue Literary Review, Midway Journal, Reed,* and elsewhere. She lives in Los Angeles where she works as a behavior analyst specializing in Autism.

J. PHILLIP WALKER was born and raised in the deep wildernesses of South Georgia where he recently graduated from the MFA program at Georgia College in May of 2012. His work has been published in Arts & Letters and Conversations Across Borders (online) with a short story forthcoming in the Fall 2014 issue of the *Carolina Review*. He currently teaches High School English in Adel, Georgia.

SUE WALKER is the Stokes Distinguished Professor of Creative Writing at the University of South Alabama (until July 31 when she will retire after 34 years of teaching.) She was the 2003 -2014 Poet Laureate of Alabama — and has published eight books of poetry, numerous anthologies, critical articles, and recently, *The Ecopoetics of James Dickey*. She is the publisher of Negative Capability Press.

WILLIAM WALSH'S books include *Speak So I Shall Know Thee: Interviews with Southern Writers, The Ordinary Life of a Sculptor, The Conscience of My Other Being, Under the Rock Umbrella: Contemporary*

American Poets from 1951-1977, and *David Bottoms: Critical Essays and Interviews*. His work has appeared in *AWP Chronicle*, *Cimarron Review*, *Five Points*, *Flannery O'Connor Review*, *The Georgia Review*, *James Dickey Review*, *The Kenyon Review*, *Michigan Quarterly Review*, *North American Review*, *Poetry Daily*, *Poets & Writers*, *Rattle*, *Shenandoah*, *Slant*, and *Valparaiso Review*.

THERESA MALPHRUS WELFORD grew up in a working-class family in Port Wentworth, Georgia, a small industrial town near her birthplace of Savannah. Theresa spent her youth cheering on the Robert W. Groves football team, driving under the influence of intoxicants and stupidity, and smoking cigarettes in disco bathrooms, while somehow earning good grades in her classes. She then went on to earn a Bachelor's Degree from the local commuter college, a Master's Degree from the University of Georgia, and, eventually, a PhD from the University of Essex (in England). She has taught writing classes at Georgia Southern University for over two decades. She has published poetry, creative nonfiction, book chapters, academic articles, and two edited collections of poetry.

JENNIFER WHEELOCK'S poems have appeared in many journals and anthologies, including *New Millennium Writings*, *The Inflectionist Review*, *River Styx*, *Garbanzo*, *North Atlantic Review*, *Atlanta Review*, *The Peralta Press*, *Comstock Review*, *The Emily Dickinson Award Anthology*, and the online journal *Blaze*. Her poem "Feeding Francis Bacon" appears in the book *Thirteen Ways of Looking for a Poem: A Guide to Writing Poetry* in the chapter on formal verse. She holds an MFA from Georgia State University and a PhD from Florida State University. After making her home in Georgia for 16 years, she recently moved to California and works at UCLA.

CAREY SCOTT WILKERSON, poet and dramatist, is author of two poetry collections, *Threading Stone* and *Ars Minotaurica*. In 2013, his play, *Seven Dreams of Falling*, premiered to rave reviews in Los Angeles, received national attention, and is published by Black Box Press. He is author of the libretto for *The Ariadne Songs*, a theatre collaboration with the composer Angela Schwickert. His plays, *Ariadne in Exile* and *The Revised Diagnosis of the Minotaur's Head* are published by by Negative Capability Press. He has twice received a Writing Fellowship from the Lillian E. Smith Center for Creative Arts and has been a guest writer at Clayton State University, the University of South Alabama, and the University of Mississippi. He holds a BA and an MA from Auburn University and an MFA from Queens University of Charlotte and is working on a PhD. He teaches at Columbus State University.

M. L. WILLIAMS is the author of the chapbook *Other Medicines* and coeditor of *How Much Earth: The Fresno Poets*, along with many anthology and journal publications. He co-emcees the Poetry Corner for the Los Angeles Times Festival of Books and teaches creative writing and contemporary literature at Valdosta State University in Georgia.

PATRICIA WILLIAMS taught at the University of Wisconsin – Stevens Point, retiring after 27 years. Her poetry has been published or is forthcoming in both online and print journals in the U.S. and England, including *Lake City Lights, Poetry Quarterly, Star*Line Journal, Camel Saloon, Stoneboat, Your Daily Poem, Fox Cry, Red Booth Review, Peninsula Pulse* and others. She is a member of the Wisconsin Fellowship of Poets and lives in the countryside with her husband.

AUSTIN WILSON was born and grew up in Waycross, Georgia, near the Okefenokee Swamp and the Georgia coast, places he often write about. His B.A. is from Valdosta State in south Georgia and his M.A. from the University of Georgia. After teaching at Georgia and what was then called Memphis State, he attended the University of South Carolina (Ph.D., 1974), where his fellow Georgian James Dickey directed his creative dissertation. His work has appeared in *Poem, Southern Humanities Review, Wind, Descant, Mississippi Review, New Orleans Review, Spillway, Bloodroot, Southern Poetry Review, Intro, Mississippi Writers: Reflections of Childhood and Youth, volumes 1 and 3, From the Green Horseshoe: Poems by James Dickey's Students,* and *Squaw Valley Poetry Anthology*. In 2009 he retired after a thirty-three year career teaching at Millsaps College in Jackson, Mississippi. He recently received a fellowship in poetry from the Mississippi Arts Commission.

LINDA WIMBERLY is an artist, musician and writer from Marietta, GA, where she teaches private music lessons in piano, voice, and guitar. She has a degree in Interdisciplinary Humanities from the University of Alabama and performed as a vocalist and guitarist for over 30 years. Linda is a former Vermont Studio Center resident in writing, and her poetry has appeared in *Kalliope, Aries,* and other journals. Her vocal and choral compositions have been used in and published for schools, churches and grief counseling centers. "Your Voice Surprised Me" was published in *Kalliope – a journal of women's literature & art*, Vol. 24, No. 1, Spring 2002.

PETE WINGARD has lived in Atlanta for 19 of the last 20 years. His work has been published in *Slant: a Journal of Poetry* and the *Atlanta Journal Constitution*.

CRYSTAL JENKINS WOODS teaches English at Columbus State University in Columbus, Georgia. She is a Hambidge Fellow and hopes one day to write a black hole. *Gravity*, her first collection of poetry, was published in 2014 by New Plains Press.

WILLIAM WRIGHT is author of seven collections of poetry: four full length books, including *Tree Heresies* (Mercer University Press), *Night Field Anecdote* (Louisiana Literature Press, 2011), *Bledsoe* (Texas Review Press, 2011), and *Dark Orchard* (Texas Review Press, 2005, winner of the Breakthrough Poetry Prize). Wright's chapbooks are *Sleep Paralysis* (Stepping Stones Press, 2012, Winner of the South Carolina Poetry Initiative Prize, selected by Kwame Dawes), *Xylem & Heartwood* (Finishing Line Press, 2013) and *The Ghost Narratives*. Wright is Series Editor and Volume Co-editor of *The Southern Poetry Anthology*, a multivolume series celebrating contemporary writing of the American South, published by Texas Review Press. Additionally Wright serves as a contributing editor for *Shenandoah*, translates German poetry, and is editing three volumes, including *Hard Lines: Rough South Poetry* (with Daniel Cross Turner). Wright won the 2012 Porter Fleming Prize in Literature. Wright has recently published in *The Kenyon Review*, *Oxford American*, *The Antioch Review*, *Shenandoah*, and *Southern Poetry Review*.

KEVIN YOUNG is the author of eight books of poetry, most recently *Book of Hours*, which was featured on NPR's "Fresh Air," and editor of eight others. His previous book *Ardency: A Chronicle of the Amistad Rebels* won a 2012 American Book Award and *Jelly Roll: A Blues* was a finalist for the National Book Award and the Los Angeles Times Book Prize and winner of the Paterson Poetry Prize. His book *The Grey Album: On the Blackness of Blackness* won the Graywolf Nonfiction Prize, was a New York Times Notable Book for 2012, a finalist for the National Book Critics Circle Award for criticism, and winner of the PEN Open Award. *The Collected Poems of Lucille Clifton* (edited with Michael S. Glaser) won a Hurston-Wright Legacy Award in poetry. He is currently Atticus Haygood Professor of Creative Writing and English and curator of Literary Collections and the Raymond Danowski Poetry Library at Emory University in Atlanta. "Whole Hog, In Memoriam Jake Adam York" first appeared in the Winter Reading issue (#50) of the Southern Foodways Alliance quarterly, "Gravy."

ANDREW ZAWACKI is the author of the poetry books *Videotape* (Counterpath, 2013), *Petals of Zero Petals of One* (Talisman House, 2009), *Anabranch* (Wesleyan, 2004), and *By Reason of Breakings* (Georgia, 2002). His translation of Sébastien Smirou, *My Lorenzo* (Burning Deck, 2012), received a French Voices Grant, while his translation of Smirou's *See About,* forthcoming from La Presse, earned an NEA Translation Fellowship. A former fellow of the Slovenian Writers' Association, Zawacki edited *Afterwards: Slovenian Writing 1945-1995* (White Pine, 1999) and edited and co-translated Aleš Debeljak's *Without Anesthesia: New and Selected Poems* (Persea, 2011). Notes and acknowledgments for "Georgia": After Philippe Soupault, the poem also cites Maurice Blanchot, *L'Attente l'oubli*; Louis Zukofsky, *"A"-22*; William Carlos Williams, "The Descent of Winter" (12/2); Carson McCullers, "A Tree, a Rock, a Cloud"; and Charles Olson, *The Maximus Poems: Volume Three*. Published in *Petals of Zero Petals of One* (2009), "Georgia" is reprinted here with the permission of Talisman House, Publishers, and the author. Co-winner of the 1913 Prize, the poem first appeared in *1913: a journal of forms*. It was subsequently printed as a limited-edition chapbook by Scary Topiary and Katalanché Press.

REBECCA ZIEGLER is a librarian at Georgia Southern University who keeps writing verse and striving to earn the title, poet.

ANNUAL SPONSORS

EDITOR'S CIRCLE
Dr. Charles & Mary Rodning
Drs. Ron & Sue Walker
James & Megan Honea
Barry Marks, Esq.

SUSTAINING SPONSORS
Dr. Vivian Shipley

SUPPORTING SPONSORS
Steve & Dora Rubin

CONTRIBUTING SPONSORS
Nicole Amare
Dr. Betty Ruth Speir
Phyllis Feibelman
Harry & Dorothy Riddick

ABOUT SPONSORSHIP

Since 1981 Negative Capability Press has been committed to publishing quality books of exciting and innovative poetry, fiction, and nonfiction. We are a 501(c)(3) tax-exempt nonprofit organization and are designated by the State of Alabama as a Domestic Nonprofit Corporation. Our press is managed by a volunteer collective dedicated to independent publishing. Every dollar we earn is put directly back into our press – whether it is publishing our next book, marketing our authors, maintaining our website or increasing our distribution opportunities. It is you, our valued supporters, that will allow us to continue to publish beautiful, innovative books by amazing authors. We appreciate your support!

ANNUAL SPONSORSHIP LEVELS

Contributing Sponsor - $50–$99 per year
Acknowledged on our website and in our publications.

Supporting Sponsor - $100–$249 per year
Acknowledgment, plus a limited edition broadside.

Sustaining Sponsor - $250–$499 per year
Acknowledgment, limited edition broadside, plus a signed book.

Editor's Circle - $500 and up
Acknowledgment, limited edition broadside, signed book and an invitation to our salon readings.

Donations may be made at www.negativecapabilitypress.org/donate
or by sending a check to:
Negative Capability Press, 62 Ridgelawn Dr. E, Mobile, AL 36608

RECENT & UPCOMING TITLES

Find these titles and browse our entire catalog at
www.negativecapabilitypress.org

A Day Like Today
Barbara Henning

Clutching Lambs
Janet Passehl

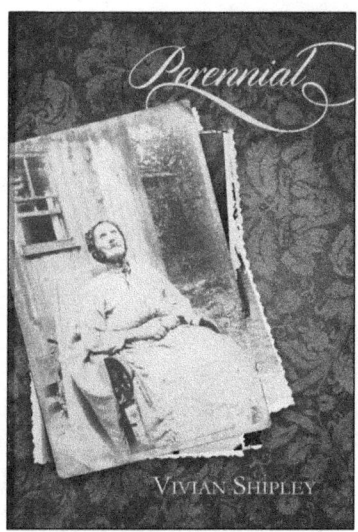

Perennial
Vivian Shipley

***Negative Capability V.34:
The Body in D[ist]ress***

www.ingramcontent.com/pod-product-compliance
Lightning Source LLC
Chambersburg PA
CBHW080411170426
43194CB00015B/2780